About the Author

Pamela Loera Moreno is a young author in her twenties, recently transformed and reborn in the name of God; she wishes to share His goodness with all. You can often find her at home, either studying, reading, or writing, bathing under the Mexican sun. Her passions include blogging about God's Word and The Visual Art around her. The written word plays an integral part in her life; she wishes to use it for good and influence those around her.

Before Him

Pamela L. M.

Before Him

Vanguard Press

VANGUARD PAPERBACK

© Copyright 2024
Pamela L. M.

The right of Pamela L. M. to be identified as author of
this work has been asserted by her in accordance with the
Copyright, Designs and Patents Act 1988.

All Rights Reserved

No reproduction, copy or transmission of this publication
may be made without written permission.
No paragraph of this publication may be reproduced,
copied or transmitted save with the written permission of the
publisher, or in accordance with the provisions
of the Copyright Act 1956 (as amended).

Any person who commits any unauthorised act in relation to
this publication may be liable to criminal
prosecution and civil claims for damages.

A CIP catalogue record for this title is
available from the British Library.

ISBN 978 1 83794 066 0

*Vanguard Press is an imprint of
Pegasus Elliot Mackenzie Publishers Ltd.*
www.pegasuspublishers.com

First Published in 2024

**Vanguard Press
Sheraton House Castle Park
Cambridge England**

Printed & Bound in Great Britain

To everyone searching for themselves who have not found who they are. May you know life is a journey and sometimes you keep finding new versions of yourself along the way.

Special thanks: To my parents who have always been my biggest supporters, being an incredible example of God's love and for giving me time to heal. To my sister for always being there to listen to me. To God, for all the ways His love has surrounded me and for His continued patience with me as I walk with Him.

BEFORE

1999 – 2007

My childhood was, without a doubt, happy. It was filled with wonderful people and memories, so much love and laughter. For all of those treasured moments of innocence and ingenuity I will always be thankful to my parents.

I grew up loved. Which is in itself a blessing I am so extremely floored by to this day. I mean unfortunately this is not the norm, and still God brought me into this world surrounded by love.

My parents love me, my family loves me, my friends love me. I was given gold without even knowing what it was when I arrived here on earth. My family surrounded me in love. I was taken care of; my wellbeing was a priority. If I got sick, I was taken to the doctor. When I was seriously sick, I was blessed enough to be able to afford, through my parents, to be in a hospital room.

If I loved a certain TV show my mom would buy me merch without me asking. We went to the zoo on sunny days. I could pick where to go for breakfast on the weekends. We could go celebrate children's day by going to my favourite amusement park. I even got to visit

Disneyland with my family, although much later on, our adventure had already started.

I mean I was utterly loved and blessed by God. He did not just give me my parents, but He also gave me my sister. My annoying and exasperating little sister who I would never give up in the world...most of the time. My partner in crime for the years of adventure Jesus had already set out for me. Yes, in His love Jesus had seen I needed a friend to hold onto through all the change and he gave me one in my sister and for that I will forever be thankful.

Yes, I was surrounded by love. So much of it, and I knew it but because it had been my all, I did not know how precious it was. Until it was gone.

I was born on Thursday 5th August 1999. My dad likes to jokingly tell the story like it was the world's biggest inconvenience for me to be born then, after my mom had started active labour a day before.

You see that day the Mexican football team would win one of their only victories in the sport with regards to a championship. To really top it off, the match in question had been against Brazil...foreshadowing? I don't know God works in mysterious ways and also has a great sense of humour. The point was I made my mom work for it and only came into the world after the match finished.

The day I jumped up and down inside my mom's womb was actually the same day my dad went to interview for a new job in a new city. He got the job and soon after we moved from Mexico City to a city of eternal spring.

Funny, faith begins with a journey and at the age of zero God was already taking me to new places.

We had an incredibly blessed life growing up. My parents had a great group of friends in the city, we would regularly meet up for big family barbecues. They became my chosen family; they still are. Despite the time and space, I will always consider them mine.

We grew up together, each child in those families grew together and those beautiful moments growing up, I will always cherish. Often times, we coincided in schools for certain grades...they were my world. Not just emotionally, I was genuinely convinced that they were the pillars on which the world stood.

Even more so because as the years went by, my dad's amazing work ethic and hard work bore fruit. He kept on getting promoted, we kept on moving to bigger houses within the city. We were blessed; God provided for us through my dad and life was good. No, scratch that, I was in paradise.

My life growing up, I'm sure was not only laughter and love, but that is exactly how I remember it. I'm sure like everything, it was probably bittersweet but for the most part I recall it all fondly. Sometimes, I wonder what would have happened if we had never left.

But 'what ifs' are clever little traps from the enemy designed to make you fixate in the past and stop living the present. And so now I give thanks to God, repeatedly for the way he displayed His love for me in my life way before

I even met Him. All before I had ever met Him, Jesus had already begun his work in me.

This is that story, my story. The story of a third world girl who became an expatriate child. A child who grew up travelling around the around, moving from country to country for twelve years. It's a story of pain and struggle, of losing myself. It's about how I found myself, a creation of all my experiences and not just what my passport says I am. It's messy and beautiful, it's my life and I pray that as you join me in remembering it, you too may examine your story only to realize you were made for much more. Let's begin!

The Announcement:

2006

I can't honestly tell you what the conversation entailed, not the specific words that left my parents nervous mouths as they told both my sister and I that we were moving. Not just moving but going to a whole new country.

I do recall, however, not being really phased by this statement. I remember not fully grasping what was being said. There was so much more behind the words that my parents were uttering, their body and their eyes spoke of so much more, but I had no real clue what that was. More! I was confused as to what was happening and why this particular move was going to be any different from all the other ones that we had already done within my own city.

At the age of six I distinctly remember going inside my own young memory card and consulting the list of places we had already been to. To see if I could find any with this new name: Brazil. My family, thanks be to God's amazing work ethic being strong within my dad, had landed lots of opportunities for growth. I have seen moving vans plenty of times growing up, I have moved all around our city and grown accustomed one way or another to change. But not this kind.

So far, in my young naïve mind the world spun around, not necessarily my city but the places that I frequented; Around my school and friends and the awesome family gatherings we would often have.

You couldn't have convinced me the world was bigger simply because I didn't care. I was happy being inside my own bubble of joy and happiness. Where nothing was really real for me yet and it was all a fantasy. My parents really made it all fantastical, my youth was a fairy-tale. That is what it was, in retrospect none of that had been real. I was six and had never ever faced real consequences or suffered any major disappointments, thank the Lord for that.

Well, aside from that whole hazy period in my life where I was constantly in and out of hospitals due to some liver infection I had, which I don't fully recall…I'll be completely honest and tell you that to this day that part of my life remains a mystery and I am okay with that because I still hate hospitals. I really don't like the feeling of having something hurt so badly and no one getting it or being able to help. So, living with anxiety and depression is sometimes a torture but more on that later. That is how that part of my life was, an endless unknown but persistent pain and I don't want to visit it again. So…

Anyway, omitting that part of my life that I hated, recalling my young life had been not just tainted in pink but dipped in the whole container of it. I had been happy.

But as soon as my parents told us without really telling us that we were moving again but this time to a whole new country called Brazil because dad had gotten a promotion…well to put it bluntly, things changed.

Moving: Brazil

Summer 2007

The whole move was a blur.

The actual move itself was kinda fun. We had never been on an airplane before. The idea that we would have to get on one to get to the new place that we were going to be living in seemed exciting. And I also guess that at that point I hadn't really thought that the world was so much bigger than I originally thought. I genuinely thought, and please don't laugh, that somehow the world that was mine and mine alone would somehow come along and be transported with me to this new destination.

But alas, that was not so and once we had actually landed, I think it took really little for the pink-colored glasses to come off and to realize that none of those people and places I so much loved would be there. For all intents and purposes, I felt alone, angry and cheated out of my life without any choice whatsoever.

In the first few months of our stay in the new country I would cry on my parents' lap at night and ask them why they had taken me away from my home.

I'm sorry Mom and Dad, that must have been tough, but I hope you truly understood how awfully scared I was. What I needed at that point was reassurance, maybe even a little white lie that everything would indeed be all right and that this was not the end of my joy. Yup, anxiety had already taken root in me then. But I guess because I was young and there were so many changes around all of us none of us detected it.

And well I must indeed mention that our initial arrival in the city of Sao Paulo was actually not that bad, not that bad at all. As a perk of my dad's transfer, we had been moved into the luxurious part of town for the first three months while our stuff arrived. And although now I see it was a blatant lie of how the country and culture really are, it was freaking cool living in that area for a while. The hotel had an awesome pool and jacuzzi, the streets were always cleaned, the green areas were always actually green and mowed and the stores all around were so freaking cool.

I remember being particularly obsessed with this bank and blockbuster down the street we were staying at. I would beg my mom to go out almost every day to go rent movies to watch. This had been one of the precious hobbies that remained the same here were the blockbuster aisles were my oyster and I could pick any film I wanted and watch it in my own native tongue. I loved it, especially the Scooby-doo cartoons.

During that time, the love I currently have for film and film making in general was in its gestation, films being the primary comfort I sought in those scary new days. And I am happy to report that later on, when we actually properly moved in, we had a local blockbuster too that used to be my very own happy place.

Man, what I would give to turn back the clock and go back to that street blockbuster and spend an hour hunting down the perfect movie, go next door for the perfect snacks and cross the street for some well-deserved ice creams for concluding our search. I will say though, that even though I do still think cinemas are my happy place, I've realized that I actually love stories and storytelling. I think it is the most powerfully human thing one can do. And I pray with all my being that the Lord helps me to become a storyteller, it speaks to my soul, and I do pray I can be successful in it.

Oh, so because everything was clean and shiny, I thought it was so freaking cool and I also had that childlike wonder which made learning new things not so scary but fascinating.

Illnesses and Hospitals

August - October 2007

Unfortunately, the whole hospital's shenanigans didn't stop the moment we crossed the border. I wish! No, in fact my really weak asthmatic and allergic immune system really rebelled against the change that it was living. Although I wish I didn't, I know for certain I could detail hospital waiting rooms we had to continuously visit in the first month alone because I kept catching one thing or another.

There was a lot of retching, a lot of fever and a lot of allergies which often lead to no breathing. I am quite convinced it was just my little body trying to come to terms with all the changes, plus all the shots I had taken prior to taking off. But anyway, the whole hospital stays and stuff, I think they inevitably shaped part of who I am today.

What I really hated was when my allergies would really hit up and I couldn't breathe, damn we really do take that for granted. I remember this little kid's room with paintings on all the walls, where these chairs would be set next to some nebulizers. The masks in question were the kind you put over your nose and mouth with meds in order for your lungs to open up and your body to start actually properly working. Those were some of the only times when I could take a decent nap and rest from all the pain. But the look of worry on my parents faces sucked big time.

And again, I remember my anxiety worrying over having them worrying over me. It really stinks having anxiety because your hyperactive mind is constantly looking for something to obsess about.

But thankfully today I can better cling onto what is real and not the thoughts inside my head. Even though right now as I write this, I am going through a horrible anxious episode over my fate in life, but I pray this story, my story does well and that the lord helps me find my path by sharing it.

I hated it, I didn't want to be there, and I certainly didn't want to be that tired. But anyway, the fact remained that all of these experiences inevitably would end up having me acquainted with the hospital facilities in each country I lived in. And whether I liked it or not, I think the whole idea of being a burden to my parents ended up turning me into an overly responsible older sibling. The second parent if you will. And yeah, all of that I learned now with therapy but yeah, chasing perfection not to burden your parents, I can honestly say is distressing.

And unfortunately, this is a very common symptom all of us older siblings can relate to.

Plus, the added pressure of our lifestyle became really toxic and later on this would become a massive hinderance to my wellbeing. And that is why I quickly inserted this chapter, because I do really believe that health is an antecedent of your previous behaviours.

Don't get me wrong, I don't think we are conditioned to being stuck in the past and not moving forwards towards change. My view on that is that thankfully I get to start a new day every day and that I am not only breathing a lot better now, sans all the allergies and asthma, but also being able to change, improve and grow.

I think one of life's greatest blessings is the opportunity to change and look forward to doing so. If I had simply accepted that my whole life, I was going to be in hospital rooms I would have become a victim of my own life.

Okay…What I did instead was really not the best either but hey we live, and we learn and thankfully I have. I continue to do so; I carry on learning every day and changing as I do.

Accepting that no one is ever right and leaving some grace for my own mistakes and seeing them in a new light.

Okay, okay, okay, this whole life philosophy might seem really archaic right now without an actual case study to put forwards so I will continuously return to this idea throughout the story…of my life? Basically, what I am trying to say is that currently this is my life philosophy – even though at times I struggle to follow it – and I intend to share it with you too in hopes you can grow and become exactly who you desire.

Starting at an International School

Summer 2007

A few months after the whole 'adjusting to being in a new country where my body was betraying me', not knowing anybody, it was time to start in a new school.

Back then I had never really gone to school in like a serious way, you know? I was six when we left and at that point in my life school was all fun and games and I was legit starting to learn the alphabet with all the words and stuff so I could create words. I could not build sentences or much less read well. But nah, Brazil's International educational system really showed me up.

I went into year two in an IB school which meant standards were not just higher than in the Mexican educational system, they were just higher in general.

The day my parents dropped us off in our classes I remember seeing them walk down the stairs to the exit in front of my classroom and having this resolved will inside of me that I wouldn't cry. Everything in my wanted to cry, where the heck was I? I didn't know anyone; the uniform was so dang weird, and everyone was speaking languages that I couldn't for the life of me understand.

And to add insult to injury, the people around me not only seemed perfectly capable of following what the teacher said but they had been friends for a while now and I was the outsider.

And to make it all SOOO much worse I didn't understand a lick of what they were saying. Looking back at it I can see this was my anxiety really getting the better of me because Portuguese and Spanish, well and I guess English too, have all roots in Latin so it isn't too hard to get an idea if you try. But for a seven-year-old, man was that terrifying. People around me switched from English to Portuguese with such ease it made my head spin.

The first class I spent not just reminding myself not to cry but also feeling like a total impostor. All the kids around me understood what was happening, they had no qualms writing and speaking and reading and I had no freaking idea at all what some of the letters in front of me were called or how they even sounded like in Spanish. Much less in English.

And not only that, but the math classes were also so much more advanced than were I had left off! Where I had been learning shapes and colours, they were doing basic fractions and multiplications all the way to the table of six. To say I was terrified and felt completely out of my element would have been putting it very mildly.

I also remember there being this teacher who came to ask who needed extra help and assistance in class to please come up and present themselves. Every single person turned my way and pointed at me. I vehemently shook my head, thinking somehow, despite absolutely knowing nothing and doing nothing, I was screwed.

I was terrified as she gestured for me to go over to her, speaking to me but not really making any sense. She led me out of the class of hell into what I had assumed would be the dean's office to tell my parents that it was all over. I had not just failed but I was beyond teachable; there was no way I was ever going to fit in, so they better come pick me up and leave me alone forever.

That was not it, however, and I was indeed taken aside to a little building in the middle of the school where many other kids, who like me had all types of struggles; with the language or the speed or simply needed assistance and had no way of really being in class at the same pace as the others.

I grew to love it there and I ended up spending significant amounts of tutoring with those teachers for the next three years and a half. But those moments, they were the absolute best, and it was there that my love and passion for learning grew.

These new ideas and languages no longer seemed so scary or foreign. Now all the classes were fun, and we got to learn at our own pace. Unfortunately, I don't recall the name of all the teachers who tutored me then but one. And to Mrs. T and everyone else who held my hand until I felt strong enough to venture on my own into the jungle that is school; I don't just owe you my studies and tenacity to achieve the best but so much more. You taught me to love learning and change and those are aspects of my life will always be thankful for.

You taught me to persevere and to keep trying no matter how hard things may seem. You taught me without really trying, that life is all about perspective and that no matter how different my learning style and pace might have been to my peers I was still learning. You invertedly taught me life is pretty much the same way too.

And to me that is one of the most precious lessons to have learned with you guys and I am forever grateful that I met your wonderful and beautiful souls. It is teachers like you who make the world spin, make kids laugh and grow wiser every day. You really did plant the seeds in all of us for a better future. I pray we do manage to do it and make you proud.

Books And Other Worlds:

End of School year, Summer 2008

It was at this point in my life that my love for reading began. What had once seemed like hieroglyphics to me, now represented possibilities.

I remember the year after I had come into the school, having progressed quite nicely if I do say so myself, my year 2 teacher said her farewell while handing out advice. Mrs. B congratulated me on the progress I had made and encouraged me strongly to pursue reading. To not only read, but to read aloud and to expand my vocabulary.

She handed me a list of books she recommended and while I never really got round to all of them, the ones that I did read are to this day some of the best books I have ever immersed myself in.

Yes, at the time she said it with the sole purpose to allow my communication skills to improve since I was severely lacking in that area in terms of saying more than "my name is" and "I like…" with confidence.

When I picked up Harry Potter and the Philosopher Stone, Judy Moody and Mrs. Porter books, I was set in the path of adoring fantasy and storytelling as an art form.

Peter Rabbit and his friends were some of the cutest and most endearing books to read for me, and it helped that there were drawings, so I knew what was happening. Judy Moody was the best, a girl I could totally relate to and who left me wanting to explore so much more about the idea of girl power. And Harry Potter, my experience with it deserves its own chapter.

So, when I approached my librarian, whom I had developed a great rapport with, and asked her for more books with girls like Judy, I was completely stomped when she recommended, I read the biography of Mrs. Porter.

What a shock to my system. I don't know how to explain it but in my kid logic I don't know why I had never stopped to question how things worked, I just assumed they existed and that was it.

And here was my librarian telling me that this book hadn't just appeared out of thin air one day for all of us kids to read. No, they had been the work of someone's imagination, the labour of love of someone who dreamed.

I legit saw hearts, if my pupils could turn into them, they would have. What do you mean people thought of all these amazing ideas? What? I think she saw how overwhelmingly awesome that notion had been for me and instead of handing me that biography of said author she handed me the film adaptation of her life. This too was revolutionary.

And back then I began writing short stories without knowing how much I would one day love the idea of making that my job. Crossing my fingers so this book is successful! But truly, have you ever stopped to reflect on how awesomely human story telling is? Every culture, everywhere in time, in the world has their own origin story. Storytellers are some of the world's most silent heroes and learning of them in art History was a blast!

I was obsessed with Mrs. Porter stories; she hadn't just become my hero but also my inspiration. Not only did I want to break cultural norms chasing my dreams, but I wanted a love like hers, I wanted a life like hers.

And without really knowing it either she was the precursor into my life as a strong and confident feminist. I spent the following years in school researching women who changed history and made their mark. I grew an obsession on investigating the names of those women I had never heard mentioned, the ones that had done so much but had been forgotten or cast aside by a misogynistic society.

I ended up writing essays on the likes of Florence Nightingale and Amelia Earhart, Shakira and Mulan to mention a few. Gosh I loved them all and they all made me into who I am today; each of them taught me something vital about femininity and independence, about strength and wisdom in a world dominated by men.

And from that day on, I had not only fallen in love with books and stories and magic, but I wanted to make it too. I wanted to not just read but to dream and make those dreams come to life in one way or the other. At the time I did try writing my own stories, making up my own fantasies but it would still take me some time to realize that perhaps my calling had been in there all along.

Harry Potter and Me:

Summer Holidays 2008

And lastly Harry Potter. Oh man, the love I have for the series cannot really be described. I haven't really been able to explain it to anybody yet in a proper way. So, I don't expect to do it here either, but I will try.

I am sure bullying to some degree has been experimented by everybody in the world, I was no exception. For a substantial time in my stay in Brazil I did struggle with it. And although today I see the whole ordeal with new eyes and a lot more forgiveness and love for the bully in question, the ones I do struggle to forgive are the teachers themselves.

I cannot explain to you how much confusion they caused me and how angry I am with them to this day. Now that I have what many call maturity and responsibility. While I was living the whole thing, I had erroneously placed the blame on the bully. Yes, to some extent the blame should be placed there but only to some extent. We were both children and still growing, both of us strangers to the whole expatriate dance. *They* should have done better.

The adults, the responsible ones, should have done more instead of expecting us to somehow mature and stop fighting each other. I honestly don't know how teachers operate sometimes, looking back at my life I feel like if I had seen anybody else go through what both of us were going through, I would have done everything in my power to create some distance. Not placing the two of us together in a very wrong attempt to create a bond were clearly neither party was interested. What the heck was that plan anyway? And, it wasn't like it would magically work after the umpteenth attempt, what was wrong with those teachers?

And every single time I would move up a year or go to another teacher about the troubles they would make remarks such as: "Yeah I was told about you." Or "Oh so you are the problem in X's class." And the worst of it, they didn't even look bothered to hide their preconceived notions about us. They fully displayed them and somehow got it into their minds and ours that both of us were the issue and thus deserved no sympathy in all matters about academic fairness.

I spent those years constantly having to leave class to head over to the infirmary due to sudden bouts of migraines. All my teachers hated that; I could see it in their eyes whenever I would lift my hand up between pangs of white-hot searing pain to ask for permission to leave because I just couldn't see anymore.

It truly wasn't like we were both bad students, we were really well behaved, our issues were extracurricular in nature. But no, the teachers seemed adamant in bringing those issues into the classroom to 'work through them.'

And the more their judgment permeated the air as we tried and evidently failed to do what they asked, the more anxious I grew. My young soul couldn't deal with the extent to which I held onto the pressure of having to do this; having to be good because I wanted help.

No, I needed help! I could not be a bother to them because that would make me a burden to my parents. I needed to slither through and become one of them. I had to do everything in my power to be the best because if they saw how much I tried then maybe they would help us. Help me.

But no, our attempts were invisible in their eyes and the more I vexed myself to be better the worse it got. The migraines began and even that seemed to be too much of a bother. The nurses and teachers only believed in me whenever I would be physically ill, feeling nauseous, almost passing out and sweating because I needed to push myself to constantly upstage everyone in class. Then and only then was I allowed a break. Otherwise, their icy glares showed me how much they cared about my well-being.

Now I know, the amount of stress and anxiety I was dealing with had started to take a toll on my body. I had started to keep a lot to myself to be the best at everything, eventually not asking for help became synonymous with strength and maturity for me. And since my body rightly knew this wasn't right it would rebel against me.

The migraines stayed with me for a long while after, alerts from my body to address this issue. But unfortunately, I would ignore those warnings until much, much later.

And how does the magical world of 'Harry Potter' fit into all of this?

Well simple: One of the safe zones in the school would be the library and the librarians.

One summer, Mrs. B recommended I read a list of books throughout the holidays aloud to improve my English communication skills and to expand my vocabulary. I did, well I read about five of the books but the one that spoke to me was Harry.

Harry too had to wake up and leave his life and enter a whole new one; scared that the other wizards wouldn't accept him, working hard to fit in and finding his niche. I felt very close to him.

I too had left everything I had known to become a new student in this new pretentious and expensive school where I knew nobody, where the teachers were severe and unsympathetic. A place in which I needed to work hard to fit in because it truly was a battlefield for all the students, every day.

Yep, sometimes people think that private education means that things in that school, work better. I have come to realize over the ages that the main difference in the private and public systems is that the private ones are damn good at both pretending they care and pretending they are doing something where the wrong had been signalled to.

Our Home

2007-2012

For a real long time, I would have told you if you'd asked, that I would give anything to return to Brazil. For me Sao Paulo was home, the one place where I grew nice roots, where the weather was homey, where my neighbours, the culture and the food were exquisite and eventually all the previously mentioned issues were solved by divine providence because the Lord never wishes us harm.

Yes, I held onto that pipe dream of our ideal life in Brazil for a long time after we left. And truth be told I do think to this day that part of my heart will always be found in Sao Paulo. I do think that the charms of the world, or at least of mine can be found there.

But not for this new me, the new me has lived through things, she has worked on herself, and revisited old scars made at that time to make sure that they have properly healed.

So no, now I would instead tell you fondly of the wonderful times. But before I do, I will make it clear that those feelings of love for the place may perhaps never leave me.

If there is one thing, I have learned in this journey of self-discovery known as life it is this: You need to find your place. No one else's, you alone are the only company you are constantly going to keep, make sure that you love were you hang out. If not, then truly you are just laying the foundations of misery. And at the end of the day life is about living not surviving.

Okay, now let's talk about the emotional facts of my stay in Brazil for those five years. I loved it!

My parents back then made a habit of travelling far and wide the stretch of the country in which we were residing. Wherever we were, all to make the most out of this amazing experience.

And honestly later I sort of had my 'ungrateful' child moment but at this point in my life I was still so naïve and pumped with excitement about everything to not see the charm.

My parents took me everywhere in Brazil. I ended up seeing so many wonderful places and discovering a lot of culture of the big country that is Brazil. More than that I think what really helped to broaden my perspectives and my mind into being a more receptive person was the fact that I was immersed, to a very small degree, in all the different cultures that we encountered.

We ended up having a wonderful experience with many different tribes of Indigenous people in Brazil. Partly due to my parents and traveling and partly through my school and the trips that we took to also learn more about the Indigenous people and their culture and beliefs.

Learning how they still are very much a key part in Brazil today.

Sidenote: I just think it's super important that we all recognize that we are all travellers, we are all foreigners. All the countries that we are currently in are a mixture of all our ancestors, none of us can truly say that we are fully anything unless you can trace back your entire family line to having always been from that country.

And so, for me it's super important to recognize the tribes and Indigenous people that remain in each country because they are the true owners of the land so to speak. And for Indigenous tribes in Brazil right now they're going through a very hard time defending their lands and wanting to protect the Amazon rainforest which is one of the most important rainforests in the world.

Its loss would be completely catastrophic to the biodiversity of the entire planet, and it would lead down a very bad path for humanity. Not just presently but in the future, so we should all do our best to support environmentally friendly causes as best as we can. To learn about more than simply what surrounds us because ignorance in my eyes is the worse sort of malice.

But as I was saying we actually travelled quite a lot and we met a lot of different cultures within Brazil. I tried a lot of different kinds of food, I engaged in a lot of different types of cultural practices.

Truly I have a very special place in my heart for all the times that we visited Indigenous reserves, and we were invited inside of the homes of the tribes. I don't know why but I just remember specifically this one meal that I enjoyed with the kids in the tribe, and it was the most amazing meal I can remember having.

Food has such an amazing power to connect people. Having the meal was not just delicious, but the experience itself of sitting down with the kids and just being kids…I think was one of the most beautiful things I've lived. It has marked me forever.

And that is how I know for a fact that hate is not biological, you're not born with it. You are taught to hate others. Whether that be for fear or just not understanding the other. If we learn to hate something I am sure we can learn to love too. If you have the opportunity and possibility to visit, enjoy and partake in any form of Indigenous culture practices whether that is in your country or any other, I recommend it. There's something so beautiful about recognizing the roots of a place. And further than that, I believe exposure to other things, other cultures and different people and other practices is so good for the soul.

I'm not saying you must integrate all those different ideas into your life, but it is so good to see that your idea of normal may not be the only one. It is so refreshing to trust that even if you don't conform to the norms of your culture and society there are others out there and you can create your own life.

Now as a maturing and growing woman I think there's something so incredibly beautiful in the changes and differences that exist within all of us. To me, God is everywhere, and I try to see Him even in the differences I find within myself and others. To me that means He is definitely not limited to my idea of who He is.

And by default, that also means that I am not limited by my own ideas, thoughts, fears or anxieties about who I am. I am allowed to be constantly learning and changing, to grow from what I see and experience. I am allowed to grow from my failures and not be stuck in them. We can only truly change if we know that there are other ways, and the best way to know of these different paths is to meet other people and learn new things all the time.

Life Altering Perspective

Academic Year 6 – 2011 to 2012

I would say that my conscious journey to God truly began at this point. Prior to this I had known of Him and had been taught about him at church and with my family. I do come from a very Catholic upbringing. It wasn't until this point that I started to truly understand Him better.

And that's not saying much because at this point, I was still super distant from Him compared to how I am with him today. I did not know Him yet but there was this one very key moment in my childhood when I was taken away for a class trip.

I don't really remember the minutia of it but in essence the teacher had all the students come forward and talk about their faith and their belief system and even encouraged parents to share more of their belief system by coordinating a visit to each sacred place of union for each belief system. I can't even tell you how madly interesting that whole experience was!

I had grown up believing that the only correct way to relate to God was how people in my Catholic Church had been doing it. I thought you were meant to fear Him, you were meant to bow down to Him in reverence and to basically call yourself a failure to even be near His presence. I just had a vastly different image of God than all my friends then, than what I have now.

We had a very eclectic and diverse class. I thoroughly enjoyed visiting the different sacred points of union of each of my classmates. I loved visiting the different ways in which people believed in, connected and seeing how their culture connected to their identity.

I really gained so much from that class, and I don't think I would be the person I am today if it weren't for those experiences and the classmates that I had. God intervened to divinely place all of us together, in that place and time so we would all grow and become better.

I don't know if I would be the person that I am today if it weren't for those experiences. I'm so thankful that each of us were able to just be really kind and open to visiting these different places and learning more about one another, just growing more.

This also kind of connected in a way with all the history classes of World War II, understanding the gravity of freedom of expression and understanding that we're all human was so embedded in us without us seeing how important that link was with what we were learning.

I mean they just did a phenomenal job, opening our hearts to the differences around us and not being scared or ignorant of them.

I learned about Buddhist culture and the belief system that they have, I learned about Muslim faith and how they operate in their hierarchy, I learned about Jewish belief systems and how they celebrate different milestones of the year on a different calendar.

I learned about all the other faiths in my class many of which I don't remember but I remember the experience and that will never leave me. Most importantly, that experience taught me to question my relationship with God at that point in my life. I hadn't realized that people relate to Him in vastly different ways and that there had been wars about people's preconceived notion about how you should relate to Him.

And as a young person not really understanding the gravity of war or what even causes someone to make that sort of decision; I remember just being a bit weirded out with who had made the decision for me about being a Catholic. It had been made for me. Also, who had decided that Catholics needed to relate to God the way that they had been?

Not to say it is wrong, but I just started questioning everything. So, the first droplets of holy water were poured on me that day and very slowly but surely the seed of faith that lay inside of me started to blossom. But it would take many more years for me to fully come into who I proudly am today, as a deeply loved daughter of God.

The Weight of History

I already briefly touched on World War II and how that connected to the courses on the different faiths around the world. But I do want to have a chapter set apart for what I believe is the importance of understanding world history as well as your own history.

You see I grew up learning about the history of the world; I learned about the English empire and their vast dominion around the world; I learned about the American history and how that changed history itself; I learned about the history of World War I and how that led to World War II.

And I learned that just because those horrible acts happened generations before mine, we still haven't learned, and history is still repeating itself. And I didn't understand that learning all these things would make me a much more compassionate and kinder person.

I definitely think that what truly helped me to understand it in a much more personal level instead of something that happened to someone years ago, was that I had a real good friend who is Jewish and whose late family had survived the second World War. And the pride that they had when they came to share with us about what it meant to be Jewish and their own history, the joy they held despite having lived such horrible circumstances, it definitely changed me.

Meeting someone who had a direct line to all of that suffering while personally knowing that he wasn't deserving of any of that in any way shape or form, it made me want to never ever believe the ignorant lies of fear again.

When it comes to my anxiety, I haven't been too successful, but it is a process.

History helps me to see that we are incredibly flawed humans who often make mistakes guided by our fears. And if there's one thing history in general, not just my own but the world's, has taught me: You can't make decisions in fear. They often lead to not just damage to the self but damage to others and a lot of pain.

It is my opinion that in Mexico we lack true connection and understanding of these very heavy topics. I do understand that in a way it might be pointless to teach a country that never participated in a world war about those events. But I think it's important to appreciate what others have gone through, the mistakes they made and the consequences those mistakes and decisions caused so that we may never fall into those traps ourselves.

Most significantly I think one of the most important lessons I've learned about both wars is how important it is to do something if you are able to.

For my PYP project, which is a very extensive investigation you do about a topic at elementary school level, I chose to investigate World War I and what led to World War II. I learned why it was called a world war despite me never having heard about this war in Mexico. I learned exactly how damaging this first war was and how incredibly related it was to what happened in World War II. But most importantly I learned about how it takes a lot of people not doing anything for something as big and horrible as World War II to happen.

I'm not going to talk for Mexico or for any other country that I've lived in because I don't have the capacity and I also I'm not part of the military in any way shape or form. As someone who has been greatly exposed to content created during these two wars, as someone who has merely read about the nightmare that it was to live those experiences, I do want to comment on my view of what is happening in the world right now:

As I write this, Russia carries on to wage war against Ukraine, whatever excuse or reason Russia might give towards the horrible acts that they are perpetrating against Ukraine are never going to be good enough. It is my belief that no country's leader should ever make the decision to wage war on another simply due to a misunderstanding or having opposing views.

I also understand that there is a certain element of danger in other countries participating in this war, that's why Ukraine has sort of been left alone for the most part to deal with this war. I really hope that we all learn from our mistakes and if the stakes worsen, that we may all intervene in some shape or form.

And you know, I do pray that this war is over as soon as possible and that we can all learn from this too and not make these same mistakes ever again.

The fact of the matter is that as long as we are here as a species, the human race will always have to deal with some level of injustice or ignorance because we are inherently flawed.

The good thing is, as I mentioned, that we can learn, and we can grow. Change is a natural part of life, just look at nature and how it never remains static. So next time you see something that is not right, do something.

Small acts, no matter how small will make an impact. Even if it's just teaching your friends and family about something new you learned. This still gets the ball rolling and at the end of the day, my faith tells me that anyway Gods will, will be the one happening. But I would like to think we are all helping along to make that awesomely good, perfect and kind will to come to fruition.

Moving Away

Summer 2012

Five years, that was the time that we got to live in what I can honestly say is one of the most beautiful countries in the world. We were incredibly blessed, the friendships we formed were so special. The people that we met really made us not just feel welcomed but also made what had once been a foreign country feel like home.

The memories I hold from that place are so incredibly special to me and I cherish them so much for always. They helped make me into who I am today, someone who for the longest time struggled with identity issues.

You see the issue with being an expat kid, one who had the opportunity to move as much as I did, is that as a child you become very confused about who exactly you are. For the longest time if you asked me, I would have told you I was Brazilian. That's how I identified not because I didn't love Mexico but because I simply didn't know what being Mexican meant.

My life had been built in Brazil, with the people and places I had grown up with.

So even though I knew that my passport said I was Mexican I did not feel it. Further than that, I could not comfortably call myself Mexican simply because I did not feel like I had anything in common with all my Mexican family and friends. I did not and to this day don't really like Mexican food, I don't know most of our practices, I don't get the idiosyncrasies or idioms of my people. I definitely don't understand our culture fully.

I mean, eventually I grew and came to understand that your identity is your own and no one else can dictate it for you. And yes, now I can proudly say I am Mexican, and I do think that my country is pretty awesome despite its flaws.

More than that I am a deeply loved daughter of God and being His has been a blessing in all this confusion.

It is my opinion that expat kids suffer from what I will call the expat child syndrome. Which is a real syndrome, not specific to any age, where one emotionally suffers after a move abroad [1]. It's not like I was miserable all the time, only at the beginning while I was getting relocated and finding my place.

But truly I think it refers more to the mental state of the kid in the long term. I haven't read too much on it so I can't say exactly how it is, but the thing is that for sure I could see how not just me but other kids around me

---

[1] https://www.allianzcare.com/en/about-us/blog/2019/08/expat-child-syndrome.html#:~:text=Expat%20child%20syndrome%20is%20a,adolescence%20tend%20to%20suffer%20most.

struggled to understand where they belonged. And the fact that I went to an international school were all the other kids were not even natives from the country we were in, kind of made the whole thing more confusing.

I will mention that Brazil was a singular experience all on its own not just for this specific issue but because even though it was indeed an international school, there seemed to be a lot more pressure from peers and teachers to speak Portuguese rather than English.

Even though all the classes were in English, once outside of the class everyone spoke Portuguese amongst themselves. And so that got even more confusing in my little young head because I knew English for school, Portuguese to socialize and live and I had to speak Spanish with my parents at home and whenever we visited Mexico.

To be completely honest with you, I truly only began learning to speak Spanish at a competent level once I was older. More so now that I have moved back home with my parents since the beginning of the pandemic. Prior to that I had been juggling words in multiple languages to communicate my needs. I created my own language which was the amalgamation of all the ones I knew and that was how I was happy expressing myself at home. Without the pressure of having to cater to only one language.

And to be honest, today at home we still talk like that, we mix and match words from all the languages we learned and that is our normal. And I love it, I think we are so incredibly blessed to have become the family unit that we are today and that the Lord gave us the opportunity to learn all those different languages.

It was painful leaving it, the home I had built there with the people that had helped me build it. More so because for the longest time my parents had held on to the hope that we would stay there.

In the end life carries on and my dad had been offered a new opportunity in Paris. And yes, any sane person I know would have jumped at the opportunity of going to live in Paris, I must admit the idea sounds very appealing. The reality of it will come in the next part.

The truth is that at that point in my life, telling me I had to leave again after all the effort and struggle I had put into building my home felt a bit like being punched in the face. This time around I did understand what the move implied, I understood what it meant to be leaving a place now and beginning anew.

I began to understand too that a home is not a place but the feeling that you create with the people you love. My family soon became and still are to this day my home, they are the most important people in my life. I owe them all for who I am and who I want to be. I love them beyond words can express and even though I may have periods where I take them for granted, I do make sure to tell God how incredibly thankful I am that He chose them for me every day.

Brazil was wonderful and it really build me up, it marked me for life and the people that I met there will always hold such a special place in my heart. I do hope in the future I can visit again with new eyes and with the desire to learn more. I also hope I may do it with my family and or the people I love, because if there is one thing that I for sure learned is that life is meant to be shared. Not to be done alone, we were made to be companions of one another and even though at times my anxiety makes me forget this, I do intend on making that my life's goal.

To share as much as I can about life with others. I mean I am writing this book; I am writing my experiences in the hope that you may learn from this in any small way possible. More so I do hope this inspires you, to take life and do with it what you will. Life is short whilst also being really long, it's also an adventure and I know for a fact the Lord wishes you to enjoy it.

For me, remembering this is so important because it allows me to leave my episodes of anxiety and depression because I know that even though life might be confusing, painful and hard sometimes, He wants me to thrive. And if the creator of heaven and earth, the stars and sky wants me joyful, then I know for sure I can find a way.

Moving: Paris

Summer 2012

Actually, moving to Paris was a big ordeal.

I don't recall exactly what the issue was, but the deal was that our documentation was not being processed quickly enough. There was this weirdly awkward period between leaving our house and taking the plane across the Atlantic where we stayed in a hotel with very few belongings because everything had been packed and everything was moving in a boat across the sea. It was a weird time.

What I do recall though, was making the most of that time and enjoying not doing anything. After all the hassle with school and moving and the pressure of life I had, it had been nice to not really have any responsibilities or pressures. The only concern I had was being able to get my 'Turma da Monica' (Monica's gang) comics. And yeah, I absolutely love them to this day, but I can't really find them here in Mexico, so I make sure to ask for them if anyone I know is going over to Brazil.

But yeah, during that awkward period of time school had already begun in Paris and things were already taking their course.

The weirdest bit for me was the fact that one of my school mates from my previous school was actually also moving to Paris and going to the same school I was going to. We weren't friends but knowing they were already there and integrating was sort of reassuring because there would at least be one known face in the crowd.

But yeah, it was just an awkward period of waiting and trying as best as we could to enjoy the last few days we had in Brazil. It really was an 'enjoy the moment' sort of time because we were fully aware that the gift of that time was about to finish, and we would be embarking on a whole new adventure.

By this time, I had already been in airplanes plenty of time, and the good thing was that they hadn't been too long of rides. I also think at that time I did not understand the phenomenon that was flying so I hadn't been too scared.

That changed the moment I got on the plane to Paris. That was the longest plane ride I had taken on that date and I kind of hated it. Not because I was scared, not yet. It was because there really is nothing to do on a plane. My sister wrote a hilarious poem on her blackberry about the boredom I hope she shares someday. You are just left to your own thoughts.

I spent the entire trip towards my new home just spiralling down a rabbit hole of doom. One where absolutely everything would go wrong. Thankfully, that was not the case but oh boy did I believe it with conviction on the plane and as I landed on French soil.

I can recall quite clearly that when we landed my parents told both Astrid and I (my sister, whom I haven't introduced yet, but she is an important character in my life) to take our money to exchange to Euros.

Okay, again sorry to be naïve and ignorant but like, I had not stopped to think before this that every country has its own currency and that the value of each country's currency is different for each country. Why the heck do we do this to ourselves?

Money is a construct, and we place so much value on it, I know trust me I have been going through a meltdown about how I am going to make a living when all I am good at is telling stories. Hence, why I am giving writing this book a real try and praying with all of me that it works out. But yeah, we are the only species on this planet that pays to live. And that is bonkers but yeah, I kind of get the whole stressing over it. I can't wait to be in heaven where money is no object because being with God is all you need.

Next up, we travelled to the outskirts of Paris, to a small town along the Seine were many artists of the impressionist era sat by the river and painted…and made history. It was, without a doubt, one of the most historically filled places I have lived in and that is super awesome.

When we arrived, our things had not yet made its way all the way to France. So, we were put in an apartment in the centre of town, in our quaint and magically Parisian little town that I loved. Yes, the town that we ended up in was perfect and honestly, I miss the cute Parisian vibes at times, but it was still not my favourite place to live in, but it is close to the top.

It was a process adapting to a new culture. It really was a culture shock going from Brazil which is such a warm and welcoming culture to Paris, which is cold and not very welcoming. I think the Parisians have a fame for not being very nice and while this is not true for everyone, it was kind of the general conception while I was there. While we were there the president issued a public message for Parisian tourist workers to please be kinder to the tourists.

So yeah, it was a big change. Not just because of the culture and people but also because it was the first time, I went from being in a developing or third world country to a European country. Which in itself, Europe is one of the most well-off regions in the world so yeah it was a bit of a contrast.

I think a lot of European people take for granted the infrastructure of their countries and don't really question or analyse how it is that others have it. And for me that had been sort of the case. I had only known what the infrastructure of developing countries was like; cracked pavement and long lines in public hospitals to take your flu shots.

Paris was a whole other world. Beginning with the fact that the streets, despite not really been clean, were whole. There were no massive potholes all over the streets.

The public transportation was functional and preferable to private transportation. And lastly, culture and art played a really big role in people's interaction.

I guess the last one goes without saying it since it is universally known as one of the capitals of art. But yeah, art is everywhere in Paris, and I guess if you feel like art speaks to your soul, I will indeed recommend you visit.

Living...well I guess the grass is indeed greener on the other side.

Yes, the museums and historically important locations are exquisite to visit, and I think it holds so much precious and important history. I really do think that the best and most correct way to enjoy Paris is by doing some prior research on its whole history, what important roles it has played in international history, as well as all the important figures from there.

For example, I would recommend examining a brief history of the French Revolution all the way to the American independence because it is simply fascinating to see the link between both of those events. And the French constitution and its conception is one of the most fascinating pieces of written art and politics ever created. But all of that I learned way later, while in university so I was lacking all of that understanding when I lived there.

Yeah, I understood it was cool. Plus visiting the monuments and eating the French delicacies on weekends was just great.

The Dreaded Period

2012

Okay, so as I mentioned, the whole experience of moving is always stressful. Add on the fact that we moved to a whole new continent and across the sea, the furthest away we had ever been from Mexico. Add on the fact that I felt like I was not actually in a real place but a movie for the first couple of months simply because Paris was so different from everything I had known.

Okay so that kind of set the mood.

Now…there comes a time in every young ciswoman's life when womanhood really slaps you in the face as a welcome to a lifelong path of pain. You see I had not, until that point in life, really stopped to examine the differences between the sexes. To me there really weren't any other than maybe the way we called ourselves and our pronouns, the ideas of gendered clothes or anything of the sort had never really been put forwards to me. So, in my head there really were no big differences between us.

But oh boy was I wrong. I remember the whole night it happened, exactly from the moment I found the dreadful spots on my underwear to the immediate feeling of fear that engulfed me. I mean I was not ignorant; I had learned about periods in biology class, but I had not known anyone who had it. I guess I had never really talked about it with my mom either, so when it finally arrived, I felt like that was it for me.

My time being a kid was over and now I was to be a woman. I felt immediately like crying because I felt like being a kid thus far had already been hard and I couldn't fathom what being a woman would be like. I mean in general I think all adults can agree that adulting is hard.

Alas, it was not true. I was still allowed to be a child, and the good news was that today, as a child of God I am still allowed to act like one at times and that is so refreshing.

But yes, the night my good old frenemy the period came to visit me for the first time, a whole new side of me awakened to life. For the first time in my life, I started to look at myself as a person who had her own interests and that would eventually become an individual. It was revolutionary to understand that we all age, and that as we age, we change into different versions of ourselves.

At school it had been the first time that crushes and 'boyfriends' were being had. I had not, in any way shape or form, before that, ever looked at another person as if there could be something more than a friendship. To me, the concept of a 'boyfriend' seemed fascinating. I honestly think that even then we were too young to be searching for that, at least I was for sure. But not wanting to be left behind and scared of not fitting in I soon too was on the hunt for all those experiences.

I won't share more than that but yeah, I don't know what I was doing because I was definitely not ready. I barely knew who I was, and I definitely had not known myself enough to know that so yeah, I simply encourage all parents to younglings to stop and help them reflect whether the decisions they make are what they want or just due to peer pressure.

Emotional growth stump aside, I think at least for my generation there seemed to be this incredibly urge to grow up and to become adults without understanding what it truly meant to be one. And I remember chatting with my peers and having recycled conversations about what lay waiting outside of school for us.

No, I am not saying having hopes and aspirations is wrong. But I do think that it is unfortunate that teachers themselves are always telling us that school is a means to an end. A training ground for what university will be like in the future. We are encouraged to compete with one another to obtain the best grade or to be the perfect student and we are rarely encouraged to just be present and enjoy being young. And I think that's so sad.

Now as an actual adult I wish I could talk to my younger self and tell her to stop worrying so much about the perfect grades. To stop worrying about being and doing my best because life is about enjoying it. Especially when you are young and as blessed as I was, ignorant of all the real issues of life. Yes, grades are important, school is important, but life is the in between moments and I pray you do live many of them.

I do hope that if you yourself have a child or are a young person that you may hold tight to your youth. Understand that when people say school was the best time of their life's they don't mean it gets worse from then on, they simply mean that life gets more real. The worries of life become real and the expectations and demands of the world begin coming to you all at once without filters like when we were at school. Enjoy the moment, hold on to what you have today because we truly don't know what tomorrow may bring. And as long as there is breath in our lungs and hope in our hearts we should learn to enjoy and appreciate every moment.

The Big House

Once our stuff arrived it was time for us to move to our big house.

I do think to this day that our home in Paris was the coolest we had ever! Not only did it have an integrated black wood library in the living room covering half of the room from floor to ceiling, but it had both a basement and an attic. And to my parents' delight it even had a wine cellar. To my sisters and my own delight, we had both a front and back yard ample enough for our shenanigans. So yeah, it was awesome.

Best of all, each room had its own shower. My sister and I had to share a toilet but other than that everything else was perfect and I loved that house. And there are so many stories I can tell you about that place but I think that would need to be a whole book on itself rather than just a part so I will leave that for my vlogs on YouTube or even a future other book.

Who knows, only God will tell when I share them with the world.

It was in that house that I did the most travelling ever in my life. My parents did not wait a second and as soon as we moved into it, we were also leaving for other countries to embark on new adventures. We left for new adventures every time the school let us out for holidays, which was quite often because of the public calendar in France which is a direct consequence of the revolution and what the French fought for.

Which I must say is one of the coolest perks of living in a European country were syndicates *actually* do what they are meant to and there is more of a voice for the workers and their rights.

Regardless of me having been put into another so called 'international school,' it was really a British school that followed the French calendar. We had plenty of school holidays added to the fact that our school itself also had lots of outings and trips to engage our young minds in different forms of learning. It was the most holistic learning environment I was in of all the schools I attended but if there is one thing I know for sure, is that there is no such thing as a perfect school and there will never be. Even those amazing school grounds and program needed work and I hope today they have progressed some.

Still, I will tell you about all my adventures in this part and all that I learned from them, in a nutshell I realized that all of us are but tiny specs in the grand cosmos of history. And to me that sounds so great because no matter how much pressure I put on myself to be whoever I deem my anxiety thinks I should be, I know that people have lived before me, and they will after me.

People have lived with less and more than I have, but the key part is they have lived and not just survived so I can do it too. Not just that but I learned how each culture and generation left its mark on the world and I pray with all my being that ours leaves the right one behind for our future kids to see that we didn't add to the problems of the world but rather we tried to lessen them.

Discovering the World

As I mentioned, my parents really took the opportunity of being on the other side of the sea and just rolled with it.

They made the most out of it and as the great parents that they are they tried to pull us along to see all the amazing things this world has to offer. But it was then that both Astrid and I were going through our 'ungrateful' phase so instead of being excited about another trip abroad we were angry that we couldn't just hang out at the mall with our friends.

Yeah, in retrospect we really needed some good sense shaken into us, but everyone we knew was just other kids our age with the same issue. We felt normal complaining about those issues. Plus, now, I can see my anxiety really played front and centre then and leaving my comfort zone was just not okay with me at all. My parents called those teenage tantrums, so it really never got better.

Now I understand my dad's disappointment in us not having taken the opportunity to even roam the streets of Paris on the weekend instead of just choosing to hang out at the malls. We really failed there but hey we are only human, and I was too young to understand what exactly it was I was missing on.

England Trip

End of Academic Year 2012 to 2013

The first trip abroad I remember taking was with my school and it was to a small British island close to France by the name of Guernsey.

I understand that it was a strategic point for the second world war and the advantage that England had as an island apart from Europe, but I don't know much else about it from a Historical perspective.

Now, from personal experience I can say that trip was one of those 'I almost died, and I can't believe I am alive' sort of trips. And it wouldn't be the last but hey, if there is one good thing that comes from those moments is that you really start to count your blessings and to appreciate life.

At the end of each academic year our school would take us to some foreign country to learn about the culture. It served both as a human learning opportunity as well as a bonding exercise with our classmates. Which in retrospect was weird because it was at the end of the year and many of our peers often left on to greener pastures once all was said and done. It might have been better to do it at the start of the year but whatever.

Anyways, we went to Guernsey for a week at the end of the year and the activities were water related and or to do with the great outdoors.

We were customarily split up into groups, mixing all the classes up as well as all the pupils so that you were inevitably stuck with people you had never hung out with. But the cool thing was that after a week of gruelling torture from the outdoors we all developed new bonds and amazing memories. And all of them, including the bad ones will always have a special place in my heart, and will also be the inspiration for fantasy novels I hope to write in the future.

The whole week was an ordeal in and of itself but the most amazing and interesting anecdote I can share about the week was on the first day itself: The first full day. You see we often arrived on Sunday evenings so we could all chill and get to know the place a little with our friends before the week began. And the completely filled schedule the school had made would begin as if checking off a checklist to tell them we had indeed managed to do all the touristy activities in that destination.

The first actual full day I had been assigned to group B; I think it was composed of six kids. Three boys and three girls along with one teacher for our group and a monitor from the grounds so that we wouldn't get lost. And the first order of business was a half day long hike so that we could reach the highest point in the island by midday, have our packed lunches there and then be back so we could arrive a little way before dinner to the hotel.

As it was a hike we left from the hotel with our backpacks and our rain jackets on, because of course it was raining, and walked straight into the thick bush. And let me tell you, kids really place all their trust in adults. We assume that adults just know what they are doing, especially when you are in a foreign country with other kids your age and only two other adults with you.

Everything that could have gone wrong on that trip went wrong. I mean, walking off from the hotel with pouring rain and only our wet pants and jackets should have been a clear indicator but no. We kept on forging through; despite the thick and heavy fog, we all followed through like little ducklings behind the teacher trusting that they knew what was happening.

The first real issue arose about an hour into the hike when one of us spotted a nice-looking flower growing by the cliff and called us all over. I don't know why, and I also don't remember what the conversation was, but we all touched it. And, because it was raining so hard, we had to constantly wipe the water off our faces. That in combination with whatever toxins the flower had resulted in all of us hiking the rest of the day with swollen eyes.

It happened gradually, the swelling, and it was just us kids complained about the fog getting worse and not being able to see properly that the teacher looked at us and told us all to stop touching our faces. She had to take pictures of us to show us that indeed our eyes were almost swollen shut and from then we deduced that the only thing we had all touched was the flower. So yeah, we navigated the supposed pre-planned hike pretty much blind.

I remember one of my friends, a pessimist with lots of humour just commenting non-stop about how that was just the beginning. A couple of hours later, we all started complaining about being hungry and tired. Yes, we were young and supposedly energetic but at that point it had felt like we had been walking without a break for ages. And it also seemed like we were no closer to the highest point of the island than we had been hours before.

If anything, we felt like we were just walking aimlessly through trees, whatever clearly marked path we had been following at the beginning had been left behind hours ago and we just wanted a nice warm place to rest and eat our snack.

I think the both the teacher and monitor realized at that point that the façade they had created just needed to be torn down. And so, they revealed to us around two in the afternoon that they had no clue were in the map we were and also no clue how far off we were from the hotel. In fact, they told us that we had indeed been wandering aimlessly through the woods for a couple of hours in the hopes of finding a path but now it seemed we had gotten more lost than ever.

Now, the fact that none of this really phased us if not more so annoyed us spoke levels. Volumes about the level of trust we had with our teachers. You see, at that point we were way hungry and tired, way more than anything else. Our concern wasn't 'Oh my God, we are lost in the middle of nowhere and we will probably die!' No, our main concern was, 'So you are telling us that the nice and warm gazebo you hyped up the entire hike will indeed not be used by us?'

Somehow, we found an abandoned old war fort and made our way inside. It smelled musty and old in there but at that point we were all so hungry that we just crammed in there, sat on the floor and started devouring our food like we hadn't eaten in days. That pit stop was rather short, partly because we ate so quickly and partly because the teacher was in a rush to get us back out there so we could find our way back.

We kept on walking; at that point we had satiated our hunger but now we were just tired of the rain and slowly becoming more concerned that we wouldn't make it back to our warm and cosy hotel rooms that night.

I do remember we started to climb up a hill and all the struggle of doing so with the wet ground and the mud had as all groaning and moaning because surely the right way was down and not up. But we kept at it and through it all my pessimist friend now resolved to hypothesizing about the possible ways we would die. Its holds more humour now. While another one of us prayed aloud God would just send over a helicopter already so we could go rest. That seemed like a better response to the situation for me, so I too joined in on that prayer and asked God to consider maybe also letting us off the hook for the rest of the week.

Neither of those things happened but eventually we did make it all the way to the Guernsey Vaccination centre.

It was closed then but finally seeing another form of civilization after only seeing trees was euphoric. I don't think kids have ever cheered louder about seeing a vaccination centre than we did.

Thankfully, from there both the teacher and the monitor found our place on the map and soon enough we made our way down an actual marked path to the hotel. We were the last team to arrive, and all the teachers were worriedly waiting for us by the entrance. Many wanted to check on us to make sure we were okay, but we were angry and tired so we just beelined to our rooms. That shower was one of the most healing ones I have ever taken. But I truly only enjoyed it as such because of the horrible wet day that preceded it.

That set the tone for the rest of the week, every day held some level of danger and therefore a sort of appeal; We learned to surf with wet suits because the water was freezing, we did cliff diving, we learned to sail, and we did mountain biking.

It was gruelling exercise that left us all exhausted after having sat down behind desks for the better part of the year, but it was fun. As I said, I made great memories and even the bad moments are fun to recall now because they taught me more about myself.

You see I learned from that first day, right after we had been given the news, we were lost that I had been wired differently. While my peers sort of freaked out over the news my immediate reaction was to think what I could do to make sure they could calm down. Not the fact that I too was a kid who was kind of freaking out and scared. Not even the fact that I was tired and just wanted to go home. No, my first instinct was to try and make sure that everyone was okay.

I spent the rest of the day holding my tongue about all the things I wanted to complain about and trying to cheer everyone up as best as I could. Somewhere along the way I had wired my brain to become the peacekeeper and even though it sounds good the reality was that at that age I had no place trying to be that for others. Not especially when I needed one. But yeah, I didn't really address that until much, much later in life.

Later too I would make my way to London and my school being an English School in France indeed required lots of extracurricular trips to London from Paris.

Good thing we had the bullet train, and the trips were not too arduous. But yeah, I eventually fell in love with London, specifically with Notting Hill and I would love to live there at some point in my life. But only God can tell if that will happen, in the end I trust His will way more than mine.

That is for sure something I have come to learn the hard way, but I am glad I have learned it. This again doesn't mean I don't at time still become insistent on my will to be done despite God literally putting hurdles and lots of clear signs not to do it, but in the end after all the suffering I realize that yeah, He is always right.

Trip to The Alps

Academic Year 2014-1015

So again, one of the trips that I took was the lovely French alps.

This one was shorter than all the other ones, I think it was just over the weekend, but it was one of the most memorable ones I have ever taken. Beginning with the fact that we were scheduled to climb not just a snowy mountain but also the iceberg all the way to the top.

The walk all the way up was a test of my asthmatic lungs and it's honestly a miracle that I did not have multiple breaks to take to make sure I could make it all the way up. In the past, hikes with school trips ended with me bedridden at least for a day. But yeah, hiking on icy ground while every other peer of yours looks completely capable of doing it because they grew up doing winter sports while you grew up with summer sports just sucks. Like honestly, having to be pretty much the only one that needed assistance and lots of time to get all the way to the top sucks, literally speaking. In a metaphorical sense remember your path is your own and you shouldn't compare; in the end you will get there!

And because of my personality and who I am, that meant that I didn't want to bother anybody so I would overexert myself and my body just to be at the same pace. That was also not even the worse part for me. No, the worse part for me was the fact that I did not at all feel comfortable going up on that mountain.

Back then the school kind of made it mandatory to go on all these trips. You had to have an exceptional reason as to why you would not be able to go. In fact, the only trip I did not go to, one that was also filled with horror stories of its own leaving one of my peers without a finger after working on carving a pole, was because I got super sick, and I had a doctor's note telling the school I needed to rest. (don't worry they found his finger and he had it re-attached).

So yeah, I had to climb, that was not up to debate.

I have always feared heights and going on that trip was one of the most terrifying experiences. Not as bad as the time we went on another trip to some woods in France and again we were forced to free climb a rock wall and I started to absolute ball my eyes out and have a full fledge melt down just a meter above ground because I was sure I would fall and die. Yeah, the teacher and climbing instructors both apologized profusely to me as they tried to calm my hysterical self-down while simultaneously looking at me like I was a joke. The comfort was given just for looks and that made it worse for me because I knew it was an irrational fear, but my fear had been real just the same.

And climbing an icy mountain where the floors were slippery the whole way through despite all of us having spikes was damn right terrifying. I was holding back tears the whole trip, and only when we made it all the way to the cabin at the top, did I fully rest and allow myself out of that fight or flight reaction my body had gone into.

I was exhausted from having just climbed all the way to the top and I too felt horrible because all my peers seemed perfectly at ease with the 'small climb' and ready for the rest of the day's activities. Not me, no I was ready to just stay in the cabin for the rest of the weekend and to make my way victoriously down once the bus had arrived to pick us up. But of course, that did not happen. No, instead, I was once again forced to participate in the iceberg walks and later in the climb.

Okay so now I will say this, a very important thing I have now just recently learned, about just a month ago: No one, not even the person you love and trust the most can make decisions for you about what you like and what you want to do.

You see for me that just recently came in the form of trying to figure out what to do with my life. My parents, who love me to bits and only want the best for me, have since the moment I told them I wanted to pursue an art-related career sort of pushed me towards a more traditional path.

At first it felt like they just didn't believe in me and that they wanted to make me into small carbon copies of them. But no, I have now come to understand that they love me and want me to have a full and happy life. And their way for me to achieve that is to have a traditionally 'safe' life. A generic life because that is what worked for them, and I guess it worked super well for me too.

But you see, although I understand now that they are coming from a place of love, the issue lies in the fact that I grew up to be a little bit of a pushover. You see, I want to please everyone and when my parents told me to try a job at a call centre or accounting, I tried it. I really did, but I was not built for that. My anxiety really latched on to me then and let me know that that was not my calling. And to make matters worse I tried so hard doing something I hated to please them that by the time I finally realized that no, that is not for me I went on another spiral of 'then what am I good for?'

When the whole world tells you what you should do because they know better, and you find yourself struggling to fit that mould our automatic response is to blame ourselves. We are lacking, we are the issue. Maybe all along the mould was the issue, we are wired for change and innovation. Don't stay in the mould, break out of it, and continuously make new ones for your life and who you want to be.

All that comes from knowing yourself, knowing who you are and who you want to be.

Unfortunately for me those concepts have only just begun their gestation after years of wanting to be the perfect daughter, sister and friend. I went against all of who I am in the pursuit of the ideal of others. And I also did it now not of my own volition but after a lifetime of suffering and pain to the point where I felt I could just not do it anymore.

It's not been an easy journey since then, but I am a work in progress, and I trust God fully with my life and the path that we are going through together.

You see for me going to the Alps had been from the very beginning something I did not want to do. I had known way before I had even gotten on the bus that I would surely not enjoy it. But due to the school's demands and wanting to be the perfect student I didn't even tell my parents how I felt, I didn't complain, and I held it all in and squished it down.

That ultimately was so much more hurtful to myself than going on the trip because those fears and emotions were still in me. I had not allowed them to come out and be processed through. My body soon became a vault of all negative emotions in the foolish hope that I would just hold onto the 'good emotions' and that my life would indeed be as good as everyone said it would be if I carried on down the 'right path'.

Yeah, a very small part of me grew during that trip. The real me, she came out while vertically climbing the iceberg and having a little accident where one of our peers survived merely because we were all attached together by multiple ropes at the hips. Had it not been for that I am quite sure we would have, all of us kids, ended up growing up with a very different life lesson.

But alas, we did take the safety measures and nothing horribly bad happened, other than my anxiety really acting up and me having to literally coach myself to breath while we were climbing. Telling myself to keep it together because the shaking made me weaker, and I needed to hold on not just for me but everyone else. As soon as we landed back on solid ground, albeit still at the tippy top of the mountain, I clearly realized I did not like that one bit.

Perhaps some of you don't really understand the importance of realizing that. But to me, it was quite monumental realizing that I don't have to like, nor be okay with everything.

That my emotions, just because they are not easy to explain, don't mean they are not valid. You see even as a new Christian baby this has been hard to juggle because we are told not to trust our heart because their feeble. But you see, I don't think that is at all true. As someone who lived mostly in survival mode her whole youth in order to try and please everyone around her, I can tell you that not listening to your most important organ is definitely not the way to go.

I do think there should be a compromise between your mind and your heart. But ultimately, I do think that your heart knows you better because it is the one that is living your body and feeling all of your emotions. And ignoring it for as long as I did ultimately end up in really bad consequences for me, consequences I am still trying to overcome to this day.

Obviously when it comes to my ridiculous fears and anxieties, I totally encourage you do not listen to your heart because it's a little liar but knowing that comes with (spiritual) maturity.

And saying no to what is not good for you emotionally is just as important as saying no to what is not good for you in general. More so I would say. Saying no to others' ideas and concepts of how you should live your life gives you the one thing we are all truly able to do, which is to choose how we live our lives. Ultimately, we are here on earth to live and enjoy life and no one but God knows you exactly as you are. So, no matter how good everyone's intentions are, it is only you who can dictate what speaks to your soul and what brings you joy and happiness.

For me, the hard part has been following through after saying no. You see that is another part of the lesson, you can always say no but you must understand that all actions, even the good ones, have consequences.

So now I am working on me, I constantly pray God may transform me because for someone as lost as I am, waiting is the biggest act of faith. For someone who was constantly chasing after others' ideals it's been hard to just be still and wait for His response. The good news is that my God is never late and therefore I trust that He is too working right now despite me not feeling or seeing it. But yeah, saying no and following through with that decision is indeed hard for someone who is still learning to set limits. But it is doable and possible, remember that.

Your life is your own and no one, not even stupid school curriculums or fear of being weird should dictate how you live it. Be true to yourself and I promise you that in the end you will be much more content with the result than if you tried pleasing everyone. It may not be easy, but it will pay off.

Other Countries, A brief Summary:

Okay so if I am being honest, as I previously mentioned during this time Astrid and I were going through our ungrateful phase, so I don't exactly recall all the trips that we went too and all we visited but thankfully we did travel. God really blessed us prior to us even knowing Him. And I do think that despite me not recalling exactly all we have seen; I can tell you that all those experiences really did build me up.

For the most part, the biggest chunk of travelling I did in my life I did with my family. My parents really did a phenomenal job in working out a way for us to enjoy all that Paris had to offer, mainly the fact that Europe is really small so travelling is much more accessible than it was back in Mexico.

And seen as we didn't know how long we were even going to stay; my parents really went all out and ceased every moment. Which in itself may be a corny concept, but we should really all carpe diem.

We didn't just travel all around Europe, but we also travelled within France which is, as I mentioned, a very historically filled country. Those trips mainly consisted of us going to abandoned castles. France is filled to the brim with them which just highlights how much better royalty had it and why the French had so many revolutions. In essence that sort of consisted of the same old stories of monarchs and why they built their palaces, only a few of them I would say have a truly interesting history. But outside of France, in other countries I found that each place has a wonderful culture and history too.

And for those countries they are inherently linked with both world wars, it's not just part of their forgotten history but in fact something that they experience every day. You can see how each country adapted and formed new laws, culture and traditions in an attempt not just to rebuilt themselves but make sure that something like that would never happen again. And to me, there is a certain beauty to that, I think we should all learn from our mistakes.

The only way to do that is to actually acknowledge your failures and mistakes, not to let them rule over you and have them haunt you. No, that is just torturing yourself and if someone else or even yourself is constantly reminding you of them, that is no help. You need to acknowledge them, analyse them, and overcome them. And then you can set them free.

You also can't live life in fear of making other mistakes, the fact is that you probably will. One of the beautiful things in life is that we are here to learn, and learning implies failing. And trust me, I have done plenty of that and probably will do much more. But I rest easy knowing that God will help me see the value in those mistakes when the time comes.

Travelling everywhere we could during those years not only helped me expand my understanding of how big and vast the world is, how much has already happened and the character of humanity as a whole. But also, it allowed me to see that if there is one thing, we all have in common is that we fail.

And despite it all we still carry on; life keeps on going whether we authorize it or not. It may at times feel like a betrayal that it does so, trust me I specially hate it when I am in a funk and it seems everyone else is just thriving, getting married and living their dream. But it also means that the world doesn't stop spinning because of my failures, people still live and laugh and enjoy each day, which means I too can enjoy and partake in those things again.

I once read somewhere that anxiety is acceptance of future failures without really knowing the outcome. Living like that is not really living at all, you see for me life is going to be a process of learning to rewire my brain. To rewrite the code in me that anticipates and accepts those future mistakes, to make myself believe that life is going to hold so many more achievements than failures. But they will still be there, helping me to grow.

Ultimately that is what we are here for, to learn and not repeat the mistake of our own past. To grow together in life from what we learn and what others share with us.

History, as I have already mentioned, is in my opinion very important and can teach us so much about the how's and why's of humanity and its current state. It can also enlighten us in the differences and changes that we have taken, showing us that we are evolving. Change is the only constant, and it is necessary in order for us to survive. If humans had stayed just as they were from the beginning, as you go through history you would soon realize we would have already gone extinct.

The good news is we evolved and changed as we learned from our mistakes.

For example, many Mexican parents today say that we the youth are the crystal generation. That is because we all go to therapy and feel too much, we are just making ourselves weaker. It saddens me they think so, but I won't lie, and I'll tell you that at one point in my life I would have probably agreed.

There is this persistently wrong idea that in order to be successful you need to be independent and do life on your own. But what a lonely life that would be. Trust me I tried to live it because of the ideals of the elders around me. They don't realize however that they too need people; their afternoon tea sessions where they gossip about life is their form of therapy. The nagging depression that follows them is a result of not expressing their emotions. Their need to judge others comes from their own lack of examining themselves and their emotions. Hurt people hurt people.

I am happy to wear the label of being part of the Crystal generation, at least I am making sure that my hurt is only mine and I don't pass it on to anybody else. Generational trauma is real, and it takes one strong soul to say 'enough!' and I really hope that you and I can be those people.

Injuries

Summer 2014:

Okay so previously I had already set the stage about how horribly weak my immune system is and how I have always needed to visit the hospital for some reason or other.

Well, that did not change much when we moved to France; rather I added to my repertoire of ailments once we got there. The country in which I broke the most bones in my life was France. I don't know what to tell you because it wasn't like I was actively seeking to injure myself when I went out, but it happened.

I fractured both wrists, a couple of fingers from my right hand and ripped some ligaments on both wrists too. So yeah, no real broken bones but I did have to wear a cast on some part of my upper body for the most part in my time in France.

Funny not so funny story, the worse accident I had was falling off my bike while on a ride out with my dad and sister.

I remember it super well, all the way to the clumsy tumble that resulted in a fractured coccyx, a fractured spine, and a fractured wrist. I specially remember it because I got up super embarrassed right after the fall and pulled my bike up and limped back home. I remember walking sort of like in a trance as I held onto consciousness because my body hurt like never before and I was positive I was going to pass out. When we arrived, I laid on the sofa for a moment with my eyes closed because I had overexerted my body.

I don't know why but my family has always had a hard time accepting my pain, hence why I sometimes keep it to myself which as I already said is not good at all. But yeah, I just kept quiet and held onto my pain until the next day in school when in science class my teacher Mrs. T noticed I was actively avoiding doing certain movements and sent me straight to the nurse.

And once there she took one look at my wrist and called my parents to take me to the ER room where the tests results revealed all my ailments. I remember one of the nurses commenting how high of a pain tolerance I had since my back injuries alone should have made me pass out.

I don't know why but I took that as a compliment when in truth that should have been a warning sign for both my parents and me. What do you mean a fourteen-year-old has an incredible pain threshold? Obviously, that is not normal, no child should be awesome at dealing with pain, despite it being the sad reality of many kids around the world. Yeah, I left the hospital with not just a cast on my wrist but a weird contraption similar to a waist trainer that would naturally and slowly help my back and realign it.

And to make matters worse I was also given a donut for my fractured tail bone and told that I would forever live with it that way. As a consequence of it, I would most likely suffer pain from literally just sitting down. I was fully aware of it and did not need a doctor to tell me that because I had indeed been sitting on my butt cheeks rather than my heinie because of the pain.

What was new was the fact that it has indeed been a lifelong pain. It has gotten more manageable; the only problem arises on long rides since I can't stand sitting for longer than an hour before my whole back erupts in pain. But hey to me that is progress since in those early days, much to my chagrin, I did need the donut to be able to sit down at all.

The Winter Flu

New Year's 2016

And the flu, oh the dreaded flu. Okay so I don't know where you personally stand in the whole vaccine "debate", I do hope that you do get your shots when needed.

Let me tell you, as someone who has been consistent with her shots since a very young age, you know being prematurely born and all of the issues with my health, I have grown to appreciate the protection they give my frail body. Frail and weak indeed it is, and man was that made very clear on New Year's 2016. All of us got the Influenza and boy did it truly get us.

What was meant to be a time of hope and a new beginning, as each new year's typically is, was instead a horrible time where each of us took turns going to the kitchen to warm food for the rest of us.

I won't tell you all of it because it was honestly gross and nasty but suffice to say we spent a week bed ridden, except we never made it up the stairs and instead transformed the living room into our temporary living quarters where we would all lay in misery groaning due to the fever, body aches and nausea. It was horrible and an experience that not only made me and my whole family super conscious of taking our flu shots every season but also taught me how incredibly weak we all are.

Prior to this I had pretty much always been the one to suffer illnesses on my own. This time round my sister was the first to catch it and it slowly moved through us all. It is a revelation seeing that your parents, who in my eyes had always been strong and ready for anything, also succumbed to the virus. And the worse part was that as a virus, there was nothing we could do but wait for it to pass.

It was horrible but also a real time of bonding where we learned to really depend on one another. When one of us was feeling a little better and up for the trek to the kitchen we would depend on that person to nourish all of us.

God truly blessed me with my family, he chose exactly the right one for me and I will always be so incredibly thankful for that. And I was especially thankful for them at that time; I felt like that was the first time that we truly bonded over pain.

I think that pain is the true purifier. It allowed me to see that there was and is true love between us, that it goes so much deeper than words could ever express and for that I am thankful. The Lords love really showed through then and I am happy to report that I see it more today too. Back then, however, we had not yet developed an open dialogue about our emotions and feelings so while that lacked, I was glad of that experience for how open we were about our feelings. Our feelings on what the heck our body was going through but our true feelings, nonetheless.

Fragility, that is one of the biggest lessons I came to learn while in Paris. Not just of the self but of life and therefore how incredibly precious it is. Life is not just a gift, but it is a treasure, and we need to take care of it. Pain and suffering will always exist here on earth and even though being ignorant of it sounds great the true strength lies in forging on despite it. In allowing it to transform us and to mould us into better, more receptive people.

As someone who is currently going through an anxious episode in life right now I can for sure tell you that sometimes the best we can do for others in pain is just to be there. You see, my struggles are truly my own and are in my mind alone. I can't share them fully, no matter how hard I try with anyone else because for me to do that they would need to *be* me.

Instead, I use my words as best I can to express my worries and my needs. And in return my parents and sister help me as best they can. In the end it is indeed up to me to choose to believe their words over my worries but knowing that I am not alone because they have physically shown me their support is awesome. And when it comes to all other forms of pain that is indeed the best we can do.

Living is hard too because of its fragility, so let's help one another through it and avoid inflicting more pain and hardship on one another. Harming others is always easy, the hard part but one I really recommend is giving a helping hand.

Be that helping hand, do to others what you would like them to do with you. When you see someone in pain offer help just as you would have liked someone to have offered you when you were in pain. Remember that it is all our responsibility to collectively make the world better and to learn from our mistakes. Let's avoid more hurt and make way for a better life for our children and us.

Change is not a thing of the future; it begins now, and it begins with us. Make the most out of every day because tomorrow is not guaranteed and count all your blessings daily.

An English School in France

2012-2016

I had already previously mentioned my school but now let me truly set the scene for you. This school was founded by the British royal family for the high-class families of Britain to have a place for their kids to study when abroad.

Over the ages, the school became a sort of unofficial international school with high standards for the students. Everyone was super smart and there was an unspoken pressure from all angles for you to always surpass yourself academically. Competition was a big thing in the school with each course being divided into levels you could ascend to depending on your academic level.

I am happy to report I was in the top level for English class where we analysed literature and did some free writing every once in a while. That was my best class and in retrospect I wonder why I did not realize sooner that my calling was somewhere in that field.

I digress, the fact was that my school was posh. Full of posh, rich kids who did not really know how privileged they were. Again, let me remind you that I was not just from Mexico but had come from very humble beginnings and those humble beginnings were still very much present with me when we arrived in France. It was a bit startling, and it all made me feel a horrible impostor syndrome, especially when my peers would make plans to take the weekend off to Italy for some skiing in the winter or plan to go on their private jet some fancy place.

Not me, I was thankful we could afford to go to the cinema even though part of me dreamed that I could one day enjoy that life of luxury. The cool thing I guess was that I was able to live beside those people because of my dad's job, perk of being an expat child, and I had incredible experiences because of it.

As an outspoken British school, we did indeed follow the British curriculum and so I did begin taking my GCSE's but never finished them because I had to leave halfway through them. But yeah, my academic years in France consisted of lots of English history, which was tense when in France but hey what's life without a little danger. And lots of extracurricular trips to London so that all that we learned could be more fully engraved into our brains.

I especially enjoyed the trips we would take for my art and design courses to London where every night we would enjoy some play or other. I had the immense privilege of enjoying plays such as 39 steps, War Horse, Les Misérables, Billy Elliot and many more. And for an art student like me, each of them was a delight to watch since I had spent hours before in class analysing the hidden meanings of the words and the possible metaphors we would find once on stage. There truly is no better place in my opinion than a British theatre to enjoy the theatre; it is a singular experience of its own and I am so thankful I was able to enjoy it.

One of the cool things too was that there was a real connection between the crown and my school. Beginning with the fact that Princess Diana herself was at the inauguration of the school and ending with the fact that every time a royal visited France, odds where they would pop by our school to say hi.

I got the privilege of attending a tea party with her now royal highness Camila Parker, where the kid I was in charged off tugged on her shiny necklace making me die of shame and thanking her for being so gracious and taking it in stride.

I also met the duchess of Wessex on her visit to Paris when she came to see the school. And later on in life we actually also saw from a close distance Prince William himself. Yup, we are pretty much best friends…haha no. I do think it's such a weirdly cool experience and I am happy to have lived it.

Popularity Versus Real Friendships

Peer pressure is real, and it is a big strong entity that if you are not aware can lead to lots of damage.

Such was the case for me, not because there was one particular individual in specific that told me I had to be a certain way but because everyone around me seemed obsessed in chasing the same things. Things such as popularity, partying, coming back after the weekend with the most outrageous stories and of course, boyfriends.

You see I did for a time fall into the trap of wanting to be popular, mistaking this idea for friendships. I mean they are not mutually exclusive concepts but at least for my generation at the time it was hard for you to be able to find both at the same time.

I regret the mistakes I made, the people I hurt and the damage I caused in the pursuit of this so-called popularity. But in the end life did discipline me, quite kindly I may add, and I thankfully had my awesome friend group B.A.P.A waiting for me with open arms once I fell from my pedestal.

It was not just lonely up there, but it was miserable living there, with kids being cruel and gossiping about anything and everything. And if there was nothing new to talk about then you would make something up and that was horrible.

I particularly recall a parody my class created of a well-known song as a new form of bullying a certain individual in the class. At the time I did not see it as bullying, everyone was doing it and even though we sung it in front of the teachers we were never rebuked. But it was bullying, and it was hurtful, and I am so incredibly sorry for it. It was not just mean, but it was rude and once again I fully blame the adults for not having interceded before.

I want to take the time to apologies sincerely for any and all hurt I caused. Whether it was intentional or unintentional to everyone during that time. There is no excuse for our behaviour then, but I think the fact that we all participated in those activities spoke of some level of emotional hurt inside all of us.

There are people I owe personal apologies to, friendships I damaged that I wish I could magically repair but I sincerely hope that just like I learned from those mistakes they have too. I pray with all of me that they not just conquered those trials but that they are currently thriving.

No one is perfect, I surely am not, and my mistakes may be my own, but I did want to mention that there was a time in my youth where I just simply made all the wrong choices chasing the wrong dreams. I am sorry. You know who you are, and I hope one day we may share a laugh again.

But yes, one of the beautiful things to come out of that dreadful experience was the fact that I managed to forge some of the most awesome friendships I have ever had or ever will have. My B.A.P.A squad forged in the school gardens in a place we baptized 'the boring place' (nothing ever happened there).

We have been friends for a little over a decade and even though time and distance has made its way between us I am happy to report that I am confident that if I were ever to need them, they would show up. And to me there is no greater treasure in life than forging those types of friendships. They are part of my world, the ones that help to keep it turning and I am so incredibly happy to know them and call them my friends.

With them I have too embarked in some of the most amazing adventures, getting lost and almost dying of hypothermia in Iceland, trying edibles for the first time in Amsterdam and many more. All of them are great treasures of my life and I hold them so very closely in my heart.

They are the ones that help me gain perspective in the joys of life when my depression really grabs a hold of me. They are the best and I love them with my whole heart; I am so lucky that God chose them for me. That He placed them in the same school as me at the same time I was there, they have been one of life's greatest blessings.

Unfortunately, I did not rightly enjoy our time together because again, I was chasing popularity. But their awesomeness lay in the fact that they waited for me. Once I was done with all of that they welcomed me back in and together we made my first ever short film. It's horrible and even more horribly edited. But I loved the whole process of making it and I love seeing it for a good laugh when needed. I do think though that the idea was great so I will keep the plot to myself for now in the hopes that in the future we can perhaps remake it with not just better equipment but just above all better acting skills and a lot more laughs.

Yup, thanks Lord, you have been too kind in your blessings, but I am not complaining.

Duke of Edinburgh Award:

Weekend by End of Academic Year 2013-2014

I already mentioned that thanks to my dad's job I got to enjoy, at least on an academic level, the luxurious lifestyle of the higher-class brits.

Well one of the weird but also fascinatingly cool aspects of being in an English school was the 'Duke of Edinburgh Awards' or DOE for short. Essentially, these awards are recognitions from the crown itself on your level of wilderness and survival knowledge. The awards are split into three parts: bronze, silver and gold. I only did the Bronze. But yeah, anyway each level gets more demanding and tough and the whole idea behind it is that the school assists those interested in planning a solo trip with your peers in the wilderness with a specific goal in mind. It's not enough to simply do the trip alone, you must also do some activity or other on the trip and document it.

For example, in my group we decided we would build a shelter…horrible idea, there were other easier options available, but we somehow thought we could easily do it. Nah uh! You see all of us have come from pretty privileged lives and having to embark on a trip where you are quite literally all on your own in the wilderness is not just hard but a true test of character. My need for independence to please others was reaffirmed on the trip.

I also learned that no matter how beautiful I may find nature I am not at all a person who can be in the wild. I am a city girl through and through, I enjoy not having bugs bite me and my nice warm bed at night. The whole experience, from the practice run to the actual trip was a big event.

If there is one thing that I can assure you despite the hardships is that it was fun, it was a great bonding experience (even if it was just for the trip itself) and it really helped all of us to mature. It allowed all of us to realize and appreciate all the comforts we lived in and all that our parents and adults around us do for us.

I guess there were some useful things that came out of that such as learning to read and navigate a map. Learning to pick a good camping spot, learning to build a fire. Learning to only pack the essentials for travelling (which is just bogus by the way, there are essentials and there is comfort and I much rather be comfortable) and learning that we definitely did not know how to build a shelter out of natural resources.

The trip in question was in the French woods in the out skirts of Paris. It was nice and it showed me a different side to the dirty Parisian sidewalks. In the end I did receive my DOE award level bronze and even though it is the lowest level it is still an accomplishment in itself.

For me it allowed me to overcome lots of my fears and discomforts which shows that we are so much more capable than what we know. If you had told me on my first year in France that inside me existed someone who could venture alone on her own in the wilderness, I would have laughed at you and told you to rest a little. But I did it, I indeed ventured alone for a whole weekend in the wilderness. I learned a lot but most importantly I erroneously somehow learned that I could live on my own.

I mean you can, but I don't recommend it, especially not for me. So yeah, I wish that out of all I learned from that trip, I had skipped that one class. Well, you live and learn.

Depression: Enter Stage Left.

WARNING: This chapter may contain potentially triggering topics such as talk of depression and suicide.

Okay so I have briefly mentioned my struggles with my mind all through this book; in the next part they will play a really important part.

It was here, at this precise point in my life, that depression stopped hiding and fully popped into my life. On my last year in France, I remember almost none of it. I was functioning automatically only doing things because I had to. There was no desire left in me to do anything. Life had slowly but surely started to lose its meaning for me, and I was just surviving because living was what was expected of me.

At this point, the idea of suicide had not really cemented itself in my brain, but it was there.

You see I had started to hold on to hurt, from the moment others' expectations and desires in me and teachers failed to help me in Brazil. As a result, I started to live life as my own biggest judge, nothing I ever did was ever good enough and soon enough I started to believe I would never be good enough.

The mistakes I made chasing popularity and the people I hurt just hurt me further and I did not just start to believe I was worthless, but I also started to believe I was a horrible human and hating myself. I could not stand to be on my own and I needed to constantly be in the company of others. I hated myself so much that I started to punish myself in other ways too, never allowing myself to be present and always chasing perfection.

Those years were not only horrible but incredibly lonely. And the worst part was that I had been faking being okay for so long that when things had started to truly go wrong no one noticed. Not my parents or my friends. No one noticed that I was miserable and that all of my laughs and actions were completely fake.

To me that made it all worse because I could not understand how everyone else could not see how much pain I was in, how much I hated living. My anxiety convinced me that I was and would always be broken and way beyond repair. Everything brought me misery until eventually feelings themselves started to not matter anymore.

By that point, my dad announced we would be moving, once again my emotion had been consuming me so much that I remember working overtime to simulate the emotions of those around me. I feigned being excited about the possibility of another adventure, I remember feigning sadness for leaving my friends. None of it was real and knowing that made me sadder because in me I knew that my inability to properly process those events meant that something in me was indeed broken.

I needed help but seen as I had convinced myself I could live life alone, I never asked for it; I held it all in and pretended all was well. I wish I could go back in time and tell young me that she was allowed to be miserable. That she could take her time to heal and process everything she had been holding onto for years. I wish many things had not been what they were, but we cannot change the past.

Instead, now I honour younger me as best I am able to today and I try to be true to myself. It's been a process, but I have come to learn that there are no such thing as bad or good emotions, they just are. Some of them are stronger than others, and some lead to some not very nice thoughts. But in the end sadness, anger, regret and sorrow are all normal feelings and signs of a healthy life.

I am still working on it, but I can tell you that now more than ever in my life, I have learned to cry when needed. I don't say this sadly, I say it joyfully as someone who held back tears for too long and only now has come to discover the cathartic experience it is to live through all your emotions.

Yes, pain sucks, but expressing it can be really healing and liberating. Whatever you're holding onto I pray you release it, mourn it and move on.

Moving In: Finland

Summer 2016

WARNING: This following part will contain conversation on potentially triggering topics such as depression, anxiety and suicidal ideation.

The move to Finland was, in my eyes, the easiest one we did in all our travels. I don't know if it was the fact that we were moving from one European country to another, and the distance was the shortest. Or if it simply was the fact that we had acquired practice and now we were really good and efficient in packing and unpacking.

Fact of the matter is that it was the smoothest moving operation we had since we had first left Mexico.

I mean in general my family is the type that generally overpacks, better to be safe than sorry, you know. When it first came to moving out of Mexico, we had moved everything but the walls of our house. Yeah, I guess moving pretty much entails this, but when you do it intercontinentally you slowly begin to realize that there are just some things you simply cannot take with you.

You see my parents started travelling ahead of us and scouting the houses and choosing houses so that we would have an idea of exactly how much space we would have. And the thing is too, that in each country the size of the house we could afford was completely dependent on the economy of the place.

For example, when we were in France, we enjoyed a big nice house because we were in a rural town on the outskirts of Paris. In Brazil, we also managed to have a really nice home because of the place and the economy back then. When we moved to Finland, a country that is not just small but has such a small population the house was not small but also not big. We had to leave lots of our belongings back in France as well as buy new ones for our new house.

And the thing is right, that I am sure today after the pandemic all of that has changed. I've had friends tell me about how horrible the situation is in Paris in terms of people no longer being able to afford a home and therefore the level of homelessness rising. I have heard of how the number of refugees has too risen in Finland and how shelters have long ago reached their full capacity.

In general, no one was able to fully prepare for the catastrophe that was the pandemic. As a result, many countries today are still struggling to heal, and their citizens are fighting tooth and nail just to survive. I won't lie, the situation is precarious, and I pray that soon enough we will all have an economic boom, and we will regain all we lost, such is my faith and hope in God.

But until then it has been tough and the scars that the virus has left in my country alone make me really sad.

Alas, moving to Finland back in 2015 was like landing in a beautifully pristine and clean new land.

Now, out of all of the countries that we had been in, Finland was for sure the cleanest, most well organized, economically stable country ever. Simply put Finland put all of the other countries to shame with how incredibly awesome it was, and I am sure it still is. No longer were the streets overcrowded and dirty, no longer did we struggle to communicate because everyone spoke fluent English and no longer did we have to travel far for nature. No, Finland is a whole paradise of its own, a beautiful example of how we can indeed live harmoniously with nature while still enjoying all the luxuries of technology and modernity.

Unfortunately for me I did not really get to enjoy it fully or rightly when I arrived.

You see I had been holding onto so much despair due to my anxiety as well as depression as a consequence of it that I was literally fighting for my life every day. I felt hollow and like at no point in my life I would actually be happy or feel anything other than pain. I was miserable, especially because I was trying. Darn I was trying, so damn hard every day just not to feel all the anxiousness, fear and worry.

But that's the thing about being anxious and worried and keeping it not just all to yourself but keeping it all in. It stays in. And as that anxiety in me grew and grew everyday started to not look like new possibilities but new forms of torture. And no matter how many times I tried to tell myself that life would get better that this was temporary I was so down that I just could not believe it.

It was only later on, with some forced healing that I started to enjoy life again. To enjoy the beautiful country that was Finland and to enjoy my family because as I have said I really do have the best family in the world.

First Year; The Over Achiever.

2016 - 2017

Have you ever seen the musical Dear Evan Hansen? Well for me it is one of the most gut wrenching, soul punching musicals of all time. I felt every single word Evan sung. I wanted to feel better, I wanted to not be miserable but what I truly felt was loneliness and despair.

Particularly I related the character of Alana the over achiever with issues of her own.

You see when I arrived at the new International School, I overworked myself to fit in and soon enough I became your stereotypical overachiever. Many mockingly called me teacher's pet because I just worked overtime. Not just to be great in all my studies but I would volunteer to help with everything that the school might have needed.

Rest was not an option for me, not because I wasn't tired, trust me I was. No, I just couldn't rest, my mind had been hyperactive, alive with the fears my anxiety would play up whenever I was alone. Especially those that told me over and over that I was of no use for anything, I was only a bother and eventually…that I would just do everyone a massive favour if I was just not there.

I want to take a moment to thank a certain individual who, unbeknownst to them, helped me during those awful times. The night-long conversations about everything and anything, the level of trust we built, helped me. I held on because of you. Thank you, I pray someday we find each other again.

You see at the time I did not know Jesus; I had not met him in the personal level that I do now. So even though the fear kept popping up I still held on and fought with myself every day. I overworked my body by just doing the most and being the best because if only I would achieve perfection, then I would not bother.

Maybe if I worked really hard and became the best at what I was trying then maybe I would not be a bother. I might actually be *needed*. I did everything you could imagine. Like Alana, I tried my damn hardest to make everyone see that I was perfectly okay, when I really wasn't.

Like Alana, I made sure that everyone would see that I was trying my hardest. Nothing would be done without me volunteering in some shape or form. In truth it was all an attempt to distract myself from my loneliness and misery as much as I could. If my mind was on the organization of the Christmas fair, on the graduation committee, organizing the high school ball and everything else then I had no time to think about me and how badly I felt.

Eventually all those distractions just weren't enough; soon it would only take one mean comment, and everything would come tumbling down.

Psychology Class, Meeting the Inner you:

2017 - 2018

On my second year in Finland, I began what many students around the world recognize as self-inflicted torture: The International Baccalaureate certificate.

For those of you who don't know what it is; It's essentially a really sophisticated, geek certificate that has the equivalence of at least the first year of university. You focus your studies on a specific branch you think will help you in your higher education. For example: I took film studies, psychology and…chemistry. The chemistry was honestly a bad call and just fuelled my anxiety so much more because I am not in any way shape or form a numbers or science person.

I can be, I used to be in the highest level of mathematics class, but it just stresses me out. It's fast thinking for the most part and I am a mellow it out and consider everything before moving forwards kind of gal.

I learned the hard way I am much more of a creative person. But when it came to chemistry, I would pray the ghost of Marie Currie would just possess me because nothing I was being taught would compute.

Anyways, the interesting and important bit for this story is that I took IB psychology. Which is funny because whenever I talk to my friends who are currently studying psychology in their first year in University, I understand everything they say. I know almost all the case studies and I can follow along with any discussion they have.

And honestly psychology is just such a fascinating field of study because it is not at all knowing about others but knowing about yourself. And to me there is nothing more beautiful than getting to know yourself better so that you may grow.

In the first year we sampled the classes of each course to see which would be the best fit for us. And in the sample of psychology class, we were each assigned a mental disorder and told to present it to the class. I don't recall what I did, I was operating automatically then, but I do recall this one kid's presentation on OCD down to a T.

I had never felt more identified in my life.

It was like absolutely everything my peer was listing was exactly my list of symptoms. I felt like for the first time I could maybe not just find out what was 'wrong' with me but also maybe find a cure.

At the end of the presentation, she mentioned the use of chemically prescribed drugs to help ease the symptoms in severe cases. It was sort of the first time it had occurred to me that maybe the issue was not me but my brain, my biology maybe. I know, weird distinction, but at least it validated in my eyes the need for help.

If there was something inherently wrong with my biology, then surely the only way I could fix it was with someone else's help. Right then and there I decided that as soon as the sign-up sheet for the IB courses was sent out I would sign up for psychology.

That was one of the best decisions I would ever make, despite me not wanting to study it seriously I do think it added so much. It gave me much more patience with myself and I am so thankful for that.

The second year of my Finnish adventure began, along with the very first one of my IB studies.

The psychology courses, as well as my English ones, were monumental in slowly starting to chip away at the façade I had held up for so long. The themes we discussed in English class made me fully aware of the power of words and how much they can heal and hurt. While in psychology I discovered the weird notion that absolutely everyone struggles with living.

One psychology forefather was vehemently opposed to the label 'mental disorders' and even encouraged other to call them 'problems of living.'

I felt so seen in that class. For the first time I was able to explore my emotions and feelings in my own terms. Yes, in principle, everything we did in class was just theory but for me everything we learned helped me see myself in a whole new light. It was revolutionary hearing how much society and their perception of health had impacted the overall populace's mental health.

Even more so discovering that for some weird reason Latina women seemed to be amongst those who suffered the highest level of depression. I did not look too deeply into the possible causes, but simply reading about those facts made me all the surer of the following: Maybe I did have something broken in me and maybe this wasn't as bad as I'd thought.

Maybe being broken was actually normal. Maybe whatever concept of normal I had built up, had been wrong all along and it may just be, okay to not be okay. (This by the way is absolutely true).

Those truths resonated so deeply inside of me then. I remember walking out of psychology classes a bit baffled and speechless. Wanting time to digest everything that was hitting me right in the face.

I didn't know it then, but now I know that in a very personal way, God had been talking to me. Gently humbling me, allowing me to see no one at all, especially me, could ever achieve perfection no matter how hard you try.

You see, I have always been a very cause and effect logic type of person. When I have an issue, I want to dissect the problem until I find the root of it. To me being able to locate the root of the problem means I can investigate it, study it, and eventually fix it. If I know the how and why for things, then I can make everything else work in my head.

Unfortunately for me I had been trying to apply those same steps to analysing and interacting with people. And to some degree there are times when I still do. For the most part though, I have come to understand that as the incredibly flawed humans that we are there is no way we can ever pinpoint the true root of why or how of someone's actions.

It would be ideal to sit down and examine all of your life to try to understand how you came to build your own morals. Morals which ultimately lead to how you view and behave in the world effectively giving you a how and why of you being who you are. Wouldn't that be handy? A manual for life.

The truth is life is so much more complicated and no matter what happens sometimes it doesn't just take pinpointing the issue. Sometimes life and your feelings get the better of you, like when I am in one of my anxiety or depression episodes. When I am in one of them, I swear I pray with all of me to just stop feeling so miserable.

Thankfully now I know the truth, I learned it the hard way, but I learned it. No one will ever be perfect or not broken. Everyone, absolutely everyone but Jesus himself, will always be lacking in one way or the other.

To me, listening to those words years later after everything I learned in psychology felt not just right but also like God had been all along waiting for me with big open arms. His truth had been there all along, I simply had not wanted to accept it. I had been so incredibly focused on doing things the way everyone told me, to become successful according to their norms. It had taken trying it exactly as they said without success and failing to realize maybe they didn't know either.

And only in that failure, when I had started to look around me, did I find Him. Only then did I see He had been waiting to hold me close all along and show me I did not have to do it alone. That there was and will always be a much better way *with* Him.

Jesus spoke to me in those classes. He dumbed himself down to my level and met me where I was. I was broken and unable to see much else because of how miserable I was. My brain, which had only then been working in autopilot and invested solely in still being the best, was only digesting information.

Even then, in those classes, I heard the truth: I was broken. But now, that didn't mean I needed to be alone or lonely. I could heal. I would heal but the first step I would have to take would be to recognize I indeed needed help.

Those classes, they were without a doubt the best way for God to make his way into my life. Of reaching out to me when I had been so distant not just from Him but from everyone. It was honestly like I had been alone in my own thoughts and fears for so long and out of nowhere I heard Him.

Back then I thought it was just my consciousness telling me to move, to do something.

It had been His Spirit moving in me. He showed me the way through my own language and understanding because I was so stuck in my own way to see anything else.

The patience, the kindness with which He did it astounds me because unfortunately it wasn't like I recognized Him then. No, it took a lot more for me to finally see him...but something had stirred in me then.

It would still take a couple more years for me to find Him, to meet Him and invite Him into my life.

But then, right then in those school halls and inside that psychology class, God had declared His claim on me. From that first sample class where I had finally allowed myself to listen to kindness and the possibility of hope. After all that time of being afraid and sadness rule over my life, it was then that God said, "She is mine, no one and nothing else will ever keep us apart."

And I'm so thankful for his determination, for never quitting on me and pursuing me until I finally saw him. Thankful that He still pursues me today.

And now, after finally acknowledging that indeed I am His daughter and no one and nothing could ever separate us but my own will alone...Well now when I examine my life before knowing him, fully knowing He had been there all along, I won't ever be able to put it into words how loved that makes me feel.

And it is in that love that I rest. It's the love that I cling onto desperately, in the depths of my despair when I have a trial. All the while just praying that I see and feel nothing else.

Depending on myself and my abilities alone is not just lonely but so stupid.

I can't live life alone, none of us should. We were made for company, that's why we are born into families and later work to form our own. It is why we sometimes take the wrong decisions to impress our friends and family because at the end of the day we just want love. We want to fit in, to belong to something and someone.

Independence is one of the biggest lies the world has sold. I had bought into that idea for so long and so tightly that now as I work to reprogramed myself to His truth there are times when I still return to the old norm. One I know is wrong and toxic but because it is my default it just grieves me when I heed it.

I am not alone. You are not alone.

Please know that in your very soul. Know that you are so incredibly special and loved. Know that you have a purpose, and it has been divinely chosen by our creator. Realize how incredible it is that the Lord of all creation, of heaven and earth looked at all of creation; Past, present and future, and said: "we need one of you."

The world needs one of you, you may feel lost and without a purpose. Trust me right now that is how I feel most of the day. But my hope is not in me and what I can do. My hope is in Him, in knowing that my God never fails and never makes mistakes. And if I am here, still breathing and feeling then I am also growing. I am moving towards my purpose one way or another, especially because I want to serve Him.

All of that hope came after. It is part of the divinely chosen path God had set me onto. It is part of our journey.

I won't lie and tell you it's been easy because I can assure you it most definitely hasn't. It's been an upwards climb on rough terrain but unlike the time I was lost with my peers in Guernsey, this climb I'm absolutely sure will be awesome.

Not just the journey but the destination. And the best part is that relinquishing control over the path to Jesus has been both relaxing and reassuring. If He leads me then I know we will get there, no matter how long it takes me to find out my purpose I know what is for me will find me. That is the hope I live on; I wish and pray with all my heart that one day you can enjoy it too.

Defining Moment:

August 2017

WARNING: This following part will contain conversation on potentially triggering topics such as depression, anxiety and suicidal ideation.

Returning to those halls circa end of 2017: I did mention that I was learning, and I was indeed healing. Mega slowly but the ball was rolling. Unfortunately, it kind of started a bit late. At that point I was so sensitive and so fragile that all it would take was one horrible comment to make me shatter. And that's exactly what happened.

I won't go into the details because as I work on it with God, I have come to forgive the individual as best as I can. Mainly just letting them go from my past and praying God works in them because I just don't have it in me yet to wish them well. That is still an area I am weak in but in that weakness, God has been strong. Allowing me to understand that healing takes time and patience with oneself.

Mean and cruel words were said. Some sexist remarks too for good measure.

22nd of August of 2017: I remember the date entirely, sometimes I wish I didn't. I remember trying so incredibly hard to just feel okay and not so miserable and sad that day. In the eyes of everyone around me everything was absolutely normal and okay.

I tried to be okay, I had even made lunch plans I was really looking forwards to, with my mom. Lunch was great because even though I didn't feel great just knowing my mom was there and she loved me was great. It allowed me to explore the possibility of maybe asking for help.

Still, I wasn't ready then, I had not learned how to do that then. I had no frame of reference.

I felt so defeated after lunch. For not telling her how much help I needed but before I could even wallow in those feelings those comments pinged on my phone. Hurt people hurt people. I was not just hurting then; as soon as I read those horrible words, I rushed back to school with a newfound determination in me. If I truly were all those things then wouldn't it be so much better for everyone, maybe even the world if I just left?

Receiving those horrible messages while I already felt horrible was the last straw. Before this my mind had often wandered through those not nice thoughts.

The ones that, unfortunately for me then, held some value. Wouldn't it be so much nicer to just stop feeling everything? How awesome would it be if I just stopped existing, no more worries or fears, no one telling me how wrong I was because I would simply not be. Wouldn't it just be great if I took the problem out of the equation?

Me, if I took me out of the equation?

You see the issue with anxiety and depression is: When you are anxious you only think about all the potential horrible scenarios that could happen. Combine that with depression which lies and tell you how bad it's been and is being and always will be. It leaves you little to no hope.

Even though I still had some remnants of hope in me, they were running out. You hold no love and no patience for yourself or your misery. I was convinced that I was not just the issue in my life but the lives of those around me. Everything inside of me only saw one way out. And that day, the 22nd of August, I had run out of hope for alternatives.

I was determined that the conclusion I had reached was the right one. Having found the issue, the only thing left to do was to fix it.

I arrived back at school then, a new determination in me that was eerily scary. I dropped off all my assignments to my teachers and packed everything up in my locker. I figured I didn't want whoever was stuck with cleaning it off to have too much of a mess. I figured at least my teachers could see that I had tried until the very end.

I did not write a letter, I loathed myself so much then that I honestly saw no good in anything I could say to express to my loved ones how sorry I was. For everything. How much I regretted being a burden and how much I just wanted them to move on and live life to the fullest once my presence was gone, no longer a hinderance.

Without the letter and pretty much everything else done, I made my way to the top of the building. I knew for a fact that one of the teachers with windows facing the outdoor patio always left those windows unlocked, as well as his room.

It would be so easy, no mess. One last step and everything would just stop. I would simply stop feeling.

I never made it to his room.

Once I reached the top floor another teacher came up to me and simply said something along the lines of "Isn't today a beautiful day to be alive?"

I fled from that place like my back was on fire. Without a doubt in my mind, I had known even then that God again had stepped in and was telling me to hold on. But I couldn't, not alone. I ran.

I ran all the way down to the bottom floor where the infirmary and school psychologist were.

I ran with tears threatening to spill over in heaps and my lungs were fighting to breath.

I ran all the way to the infirmary first because that was school protocol and even then, I wanted to do this one thing right.

I ran and walked right into a small toddler sprawled on the examining table crying his eyes out from a boo boo and asked with so much despair in my voice to talk to the psychologist.

I knew she saw the look in my eyes then and without skipping a beat held my hand and walked me to her office. We walked into that small office, and I sat down on the sofa across from her as the nurse walked out. Only waiting for the door to shut behind her because I knew that small kid was on the other side. Waiting until finally everything erupted out of me. Without preambles I told her then and there "If you don't help me, I will kill myself."

The dam broke loose. I started wailing and sobbing uncontrollably and without a care in the world. I had been holding onto so much sadness for so freaking long. It was all leaving me so violently.

That was my first serious melt down, I unfortunately still suffer from them but with a better mindset now. She helped me breath first, all while making the corresponding calls to get me help. She held me, held my hand in hers as I cried my eyes out just wanting to not feel anything anymore.

She didn't let go of me, didn't leave me alone at all until my parents arrived. That stunk too, that's honestly how it felt. I had wanted to just not bother them anymore and here I was, whatever I had now, making them leave their jobs and plans in the middle of the day.

I erupted into a new fit of tears when I saw them. I cried and wailed the whole day.

We left for the hospital. All I remember was looking down at my hands the whole drive and cursing myself internally for all the bother I was causing.

The whole ordeal was a blur, they did tests on me and made me answer a long form and questionnaires about my life and my emotions. I just did them because I was told to, not because I wanted. I ate what they gave me in the waiting room because they said they wanted me to. I walked and followed them around because they asked me to.

By the time I had landed inside a rehab facility I had been so down and tired of myself it was only right they left me there. I didn't even say bye to my parents.

That first night I just cried.

I cried out all the tears I had been holding with me since Brazil. I cried all those tears of pity I had for myself.

I cried because I had come to absolutely believe the lies and thought I was beyond healing. I had convinced myself this would be my life now. Being miserable and locked away forever.

Those dreadful thoughts still cling to me at times, right now as I write this book to be honest. It's horrible, feeling like there is no way out despite now knowing there always is. Did you hear that? Pain ends. You will heal.

Rehab Facility:

August 2017

God alone worked in me that night.

For the first time in between sobs, I prayed earnestly to Him. I told him how sorry I was for being a failure; sorry for all the damage I had done. Sorry for not being strong enough to do it.

I told Him to please just help me. Help me only how he knew because I obviously was wrong. I needed help.

Somehow, I slept.

I was awoken by a nurse and asked to join breakfast.

It was weird, the overwhelming peace that gripped me that morning. It was bizarre being okay after all that had come before. Well, I wasn't okay but at least I didn't feel miserable, at least I wasn't crying and at least I felt…safe.

That new safeness was weird too, it wasn't just that I felt it, but I saw it. In that centre I was surrounded by others who like me had arrived at the same flawed conclusion. All of us were healing. Sitting down at breakfast with different saddened faces all in different stages of healing was weirdly peaceful.

It felt, honestly, like I had found my people.

While in line to get my breakfast another patient had handed me a ready-made toast. Another one passed me a cup full of cold milk. A place had been left for me, despite being the last one at the table. Someone had drawn a smiley on my napkin, a crooked grin on.

I looked up at all those faces, all of them not saying a single word but all looking back at me with so much understanding. I felt their love without them ever saying a word, telling me we were on this together, we were all healing.

Fresh tears sprung into my eyes; these ones completely different from the ones I had spilled mere hours before. These tears held hope, they washed away the fears I had of never being healed. They washed away those thoughts of unworthiness because here I was, surrounded by strangers but feeling held and loved like never before.

We ate in silence, only the sound of plates and cutlery as background noise because no one there was up for much else. Occasionally, someone would say something and the rest of us would acknowledge it, but no real conversation started. My tears were condiments for my meal. They washed away all those fears as I slowly sunk into that moment.

My reception was perfect. No words were ever exchanged but the feeling of that place, God was there.

This may sound sad but to me that rehab centre will always be the most welcoming and cosy place I have experienced. I will be forever thankful not just to the nurses but the doctors too, to my fellow patients and staff.

I would never have begun healing properly if I had not been there. God truly works all things out for those that seek him.

Its bonkers how just in the right time, in my most desperate hour, God stepped in and took control of absolutely everything. He didn't just step in and rescue me from myself, He had previously stepped in and had placed me right where I needed to be: In Finland, in a country with one of the best healthcare systems in the world, in a place where the social perception of mental health was so healthy.

In a city, with a rehab centre, where He knew I could heal.

Healing

August 2017 to present day:

Healing has been an incredibly complex journey. One I am still very much in right now.

After years of making myself my own enemy learning and becoming my own friend has been hard. There have been times when it's hard to trust me. I mean ultimately, I have come to realize that without Jesus, I definitely shouldn't trust me, but even with Jesus it's been…It's a process.

I will tell you about the healing I did before I tell you more about the one I've been doing now.

I only stayed one week in the facility. I came in crying my eyes out and I left like everything had been completely fine all the time. It had been my choice to stay only that small while. In retrospect I think I should have stayed longer. I had asked for help but, in all honesty, I had not been ready to receive it.

Don't get me wrong, the week was honestly really healing in itself, and I am glad I stayed there. It was great to just be my miserable self and not have to hide it. To not have to worry about what everyone would say if I didn't show up all made up or enthusiastic. It was so freaking nice!

But the thing was I still felt chased. I felt like there was a timeline by which I had to be healed. I was hyperaware of the fact that life was carrying on outside of those walls. A life I had been very much an active part of for so long that it felt not just wrong but immoral to even be taking this time away.

I kept having this nagging sensation where I needed to show everyone that what happened wasn't actually that bad. That I was healing and that I would heal, that I could do all of that outside of the facility. I was entirely convinced that in order for me to heal properly I had to be actually living life.

To be honest that idea has been with me up until now even though I had thought I had dropped it. You see, I did not allow myself to mourn me and what I had lost during those years of misery. I did not stop to think about how freaking sad and unfair it had all been. Not by any one person in particular but in general. I should have reflected on the fact that being constantly on the chase for perfection had been an absolutely miserable way of being. Not living.

After I left the centre, they told me I would need to take mandatory therapy for the next following year at my therapists' discretion. At first, I went three times a week. Eventually over the years we reduced it to only twice a month. But in those first few weeks, I did start to see that perhaps the life I had been stuck and predisposed to live had not been the correct choice.

I specially felt it on the first attempt to go back to school after the centre. I felt so incredibly anxious the whole freaking weekend leading up to Monday. And on Monday I woke up and in me I felt with absolute certainty I should not carry on.

Not that I couldn't do it, I had after all been living that hectically toxic life for years. No. I just simply could not carry on. It could not be a choice for me because I had already seen how freaking damaging it was. That life had been lethal, it had been slowly but surely killing me.

So as the doors shut when I got on the bus that day early on in the morning, after telling myself over and over I *should* do it, I lost it. As soon as I biped myself in I broke down crying. At least everyone had the decency to turn away and let me cry as I walked to the back exit and waited for the next stop. I all but ran out of the bus as soon as we reached the next stop and sprinted back home.

I'd called my mom to tell her I was coming back. To be honest I wish she had told me to wait, to maybe go back and to actually heal. But back then my parents had had no knowledge of what mental health actually looked like. They did not understand what was wrong with me. I mean I did not know for sure what was wrong with me, it took several more years and tests for me to actually get a diagnosis.

So, in their eyes I'm sure they saw that as a hitch, not a real cause for concern. It would take much more for them to actually start to see how freaking broken I was and how much help I would need.

I forgive them. Back then I was so freaking pissed with them, so angry they couldn't see how badly I was hurting. Angry that they had not seen how I was drowning, angry because when I started resisting, they would call me out on it. Telling me I had to be better, do better, I was dropping the ball.

I mean in their eyes I went from the stereotypical perfect child who did everything and anything, to someone who barely had the will or energy to do a single thing. Yes, the contrast was night and day. But that actually took a while.

Straight after the non-accident I jumped back into my fast-paced life and carried on. And because for the next three years I did so everyone around me, including myself, got convinced I was okay. Spoiler alert, I wasn't.

I ignored my instincts, after I returned home and cried my eyes out one last time before I pulled my metaphorical breeches up and kept going. And honestly, I did it out of desperation. I had no idea what I was doing. Much less did I know what exactly the issue had been to begin with.

I was sad, yes, my depression and anxiety stayed but the therapy sessions taught me how to persevere despite them. Not to heal but to persevere…I mean it worked then. But only for that time and those circumstances.

In my head I had convinced myself that what I had experienced wasn't as big as it felt.

What absolutely didn't help and where I definitely place a big part of the blame was when I told the headmaster of the incident that broke the camel's back. It honestly should not have been a surprise at all, the individual in question had made themselves a reputation for being particularly nasty to others and teachers alike. But for some unknown and bizarre reason the headmaster refused to believe the words I had been sent.

I wish with all of me that I could have taken a screenshot of them instead of deleting them as my nurses told me when I arrived at the centre. I mean I know it had been the right call then because I kept looking at them and hating me. But a couple of weeks later with the headmaster not believing me and telling me to choose carefully how I wanted to proceed I just knew that without actual proof from my part nothing would happen.

If the headmaster had been any good at doing their job, they could have easily called the other student in question and asked to see their phone. God knows what else they would have found. But nothing happened. Well not true, something did happen. The attitude of the headmaster sent me the biggest signal yet. It told me that what I had experienced had indeed not been as bad as I thought it to be.

I had been exaggerating and now I was better. If only the headmaster was there those next couple of weeks when the individual returned and instead now carried on saying those mean comments to my face. I would leave school grounds all together, or if I could, I would just go straight to the school therapist. Eventually I got told off, not for leaving but for not taking someone with me in 'the state' I was in. It was comical really, how I was clearly not okay, but no one did anything to help me.

Now, I've forgiven the bully...I'm working to forgive the headmaster and their lack of care for the pupils. I am healing from those horrible words, not just the bully's but the ones I had called myself.

I've been reinventing myself, making better choices and becoming a better me. Someone who is so much healthier, someone who is actually joy-filled most of the time. Someone thankful and present, no longer chasing after others' ideals. That's who I have been working to be. For the most part I think I've been doing a good job, but as I mentioned I am currently in a slump, and I am relearning those same lessons again. And a few more too for good measure.

Same old Dreams, Same old Hopes:

Final year of Highschool 2017 - 2018

As I mentioned, I definitely did 'healing' the wrong way.

In my endless chase to just 'do the right thing' I returned into my life like nothing had happened. My so called 'dreams' and 'hopes' stayed the same, my routine stayed the same. My goals remained the same.

When I returned, my long and complex plan to stay in Europe and do my higher education there remained the same. Everyone else around me was doing it, everyone was telling me to do it. So, I did it. I worked and worked. I all together left my social life behind and I chased those 'dreams.'

I got into the university of my choice and some others too, I got the grades I worked for. I even got a recognition from my teachers for all the hard work I had done. At least it had not gone unseen. I did all the right things.

I even forced myself to be excited, to celebrate the fact that I had graduated and that I had entered my top choice. I forced myself to squash down all those terrible emotions of fear that where now returning. The ones that told me perhaps all of the 'right things' were not for me. I completely ignored them and forced myself to be all that everyone else was being because it seemed they were right.

I celebrated the fact that the life I had known was ending. When I think I honestly needed to cry. I needed to mourn that too because even though it had been so bad for me and my well-being, it had been my life and it was ending. It had been all I had known, my peers and friends, my teachers and those school halls had become my whole world and now I was leaving. There would be no real mark left of mine…other than my name on a commemorative plaque.

Small Peak into the Future (one year later):

In me this new fear started rising. What if this had been it? What if I had only been good at this? Instead of letting it freeze me I refused it by diving headfirst into my new studies.

University should have been fun. My first year should have been mostly fun and about making memories. Instead, I spent the whole time working my butt off. Convinced that somehow my worth was entirely linked to my grades. Convinced that it I spared one second away from my books I would not just fail but become a failure.

Time went by in the blink of an eye and without knowing it, the year had finished. Once again, I had been sucked into a soulless, joyless life and I had not seen it. I returned back home, back to my school a year later for the graduation of my dear friend. It hit me, only then after my teacher asked me "Are you happy?" Only then, only then did I realize I wasn't.

The dam I had been filling that entire year cracked and it took absolute will power not to burst into tears then. Not to break down crying the whole weekend because after all

I was there to celebrate the achievements of my friend. That weekend was not about me.

I just looked at her, at my lovely teacher and nodded, sure that if I spoke my voice would crack. I lied to everyone who asked me if I had been enjoying university life. The awesome thing about teachers like her is that they actually care. They see you, the real you and not the fake you that we often put forward to keep going. She saw me and hours later, at the celebratory party, she pulled me aside and asked me to please tell her the truth. I still held in the tears but everything else came out.

Gosh I will forever be thankful to her simply for listening. She listened to me go on and on about how freaking terrified I was. I had spent an entire year doing the 'right thing' ignoring myself and being miserable without noticing it. University life had not been what others promised. I had not made amazing new friendships; I missed my old ones. I had not made incredible memories; for the most part the last year was filled with mental images of me in the library.

Nothing had been what they told me, what they had promised me. And even though I had done exactly what they had asked of me I was so incredibly empty. Nothing but the sheets of paper with my grades in my life held any value at all.

She listened to me, my lovely, dear teacher. She listened and advised me. She pushed me to actually become who I was meant to be, in her eyes whatever I was then was not it. She told me, to keep trying, no matter how long it took but to be sure I would find her...the me I was meant to be.

But hey I am so incredibly bad at doing was actually good for me and back then it was more of a rule rather than the exception. So, despite her words resonating inside of me I did not heed them. I did not even tell her how thankful I was for them; I did not even contact her again despite telling her I would.

Instead, I called my parents that night. I locked myself in the sauna, a vital part of almost all Finnish households, and told them everything. It must have been quite a shock to them, hearing me sobbing miles away on the eve of my friend's celebration. Hearing me tell them how freaking miserable I was, how terrified I was for who I had allowed myself to carry on being. Terrified that life would carry on passing me by.

I think my exact words had been: "I am terrified that I will carry on here, doing 'all the right things' without ever feeling whole. That I will keep up this sham only to wake up one day ten years from now and see how freaking empty and sad I am."

I begged them, honest to God begged and wallowed for them to please save me. To save me from myself and the nightmare I had been stuck living in. I begged them to just please just do something, to help me. To let me come back and figure it out from there.

They told me to mull it over. My sister, bless her heart, called me and told me to just suck it up. To realize how freaking good I had it, to be living in Europe, to be studying film criticism, to have all of that.

She told me to stay.

I now know what they did, they did in love. Thinking that staying was indeed the right thing. Ultimately, they gave me the last choice. Can we guess what I did? Of course: I chose against me! That breakdown had been real, the most real I had been in years.

My emotions had been clear then, maybe everything else was horribly blank and confusing but at least I knew without any doubt that in that life I was miserable. Unfortunately for old me, I once again made all the wrong choices and I stayed.

Yes, my healing journey had begun but that day God made it clear that healing would be forever. A continuous effort in life, to enjoy it despite all the sadness.

Graduating Highschool!

Summer 2018

Summer 2018, I graduated. My friends and I enjoyed the celebratory dinner I worked so hard to organize, some of us partied together. Little did we know that morning, us sitting together in that assembly hall would be the last time we were together. Yes, the class of 2018 was done, meant to dive into the world and into newer adventures.

As an international school, it had always had students come and go. Despite all of our differences and disagreements, the hurt we might have caused one another, I can certainly tell you I loved them all. They were mine; they were my class. The people I spent a substantial amount of my life with. They were the ones that I saw from eight in the morning until six in the afternoon if not later from Monday to Saturday.

They were the ones I would whine and complain with about how much whatever class sucked that week. Among them I found the most amazing and beautiful people. I found my people, the ones that held me when I was feeling really down without them even knowing. I found those who I could surround myself with love because they were love.

They might not have called it that but the patience and care they gave me whenever I needed help because I really wasn't made for maths or chemistry, those minutes we spent together at lunch while they explained what seems so easy to them, that was love. And too soon when we were finally getting the groove of each other and enjoying life together, we were done.

I mean for the most part I had been just surviving. Not truly realizing the beautiful people that surrounded me. It's only become apparent now, after all hindsight is always 20/20. I don't think I noticed it. I don't think I realized how much I was going to miss them until we were finally there.

As we all got up when our names were being called and we walked off the stage it dawned on me. We would never ever get to enjoy life together again. We were on our own now, expected to just go forth into the world and make good with the knowledge we had been given. I almost cried but I didn't because crying was weakness.

Instead, I enjoyed the dinner that I had planned. The one that I had organized and have been stressing about for weeks on end. I sat there, those who actually cared enough to show up being fully conscious that those people I called my own would be gone by the end of the night.

Most people take for granted how awesome it is to grow up and grow old with people. Being in an international school means that once you are done, the odds are that you will never see those people again. We all left, all of us going through different corners of the world. All of us chasing our different dreams knowing that the world was so much bigger than what we saw.

Yes, knowledge can broaden your world and it's such a beautiful thing to do. But it can also make you lonely. And that night after I had had my fair share of celebrating, I realized how much of my happiness I held within those people. How much I loved some of them. How many opportunities I missed because of my misery.

Expatriate kids are crap at maintaining contact. I think maybe somebody should do a study on that. We are super bad at long-term relationships. And that's like just my own analysis of all the people I've met throughout all those years of traveling. Maybe it's just the inconsistency. The fact that we know things have to end, nothing is permanent. Why try? In the end it avoids unnecessary pain.

I haven't talked or kept up to date with all of those I wish I had. I know, I could probably text those I miss and tell them I miss them. Again, I am horrible at doing what is good for me and I am honestly too chicken to tell some of them how much I miss them, that I need them in my life. It's been too long, and it just doesn't feel right. Maybe one day I'll gain enough courage.

Anyways, I graduated. I had gotten into a college of my choice. And so, all of those plans I had previously made about that oh so far distant future, they were here now.

Moving in: The Netherlands

August 2018

The Netherlands was a singular experience like any other I've ever lived before. It wasn't just that it was my first time living alone, I just think the Netherlands it's so different from every other European country out there.

Beginning with the fact that the most common form of transportation is a cycling and ending with the fact that weed (and other drugs) are legal. Did I try them? I already said I did try something. The rest is between me and God.

But yeah, I don't know if it was bittersweet. Some parts I absolutely loved and I pray somehow God and I can work to incorporate those elements into my new life. And some parts I hated and I wish I never have to go through that again.

Disclaimer: I just want to remind everyone that this is a book about my life so all of these words you're reading are *my* opinion.

I don't know why but I just really didn't like Dutch people. Not meaning my friends, not the people I met or the ones I studied with, they were great, but they were the exception. Everyone else outside of that bubble just seemed really rude. I don't know maybe I was unlucky...most likely.

I also hated the fact that I was alone. Like really alone. My parents had returned to Mexico at this point, taking Astrid with them. Everyone else could take the weekend off to visit their family over in the next country or maybe even catch a short flight to them. Not me, my family was on the other side of the sea, miles and miles away. I was all alone and being there made it all that much clearer.

Of course, I would call, much more than your average Uni student. I am after all, a mommy's girl. But it wasn't enough. Soon enough I would find my own family, and an awesomely incredible one. I love them all so much.

First Year: Almost Quitting but Finding Jesus

2018-2019

You see as I mentioned in the last part, I spent every waking moment working my butt off to get good grades. To do all the right things everyone was telling me to do. At the end of it, I was tired, and I did not feel fulfilled at all.

In the midst of my despair my mom gave me the brilliant idea to join a church. And so, my depressed self-looked up on Google where the nearest church was. That was how I ended up in Vineyard Church on the following Sunday. I honestly had no expectations of anything, I was feeling really down, and I just thought maybe listening to someone say some nice things about life might help me.

God delivered way beyond that.

You see, all the time before, all the hurt I was causing myself; God had given me plenty of outings. Multiple times, God had allowed me to step out of those circumstances, but I could not see it. I had been so entrapped by the world and its shininess that it was only in that holy place, filled with so much love and His presence that I slowly started to let go. Let go of all the hurting and hurtful things in my life and walking towards what was actually good.

I walked inside the school auditorium which coincidentally also served as our meeting church grounds on the weekends. That first Sunday God's reception was so loving I became His then. God claimed me, boldly and obviously that day.

When I arrived, the welcoming committee by the gates greeted me with so much enthusiasm and joy, genuinely happy for me to be there. I'd told them this was my first time ever going to church, like of my own will. They were even more eager for me to join them then. They thanked me for being there, for showing up as they walked me to my seat.

My whole first year was a blur. I arrived feigning excitement which broke down as soon as my parents texted me, they were boarding to Mexico. I bawled my eyes out once more but forced myself to go for a walk after an hour of tears. On the way back I stopped by a roommate's room, we were in a student house, and the rest was history.

Living in a student house is one of life's coolest adventures. I have awesome memories I made there, moments in between all the work. Moments I am so thankful I allowed myself to enjoy. However, all of them were surrounded by numbness and I wish I could have had all of them under better circumstances.

In terms of academic studies: The first semester was hard while also being really freaking interesting. Some courses were plain boring, but they built the foundation for what I wanted to become: A film and theatre critic.

Short Film: Matryoshka 2019

So not everything was doom and gloom. In the midst of all the suffering God gave me something to hold onto, he gave me hope where it had been running out. You see in the first year of my studies I tirelessly pursued distractions via all forms of academic engagement. This ultimately led me to join my careers extracurricular committee.

In specific I became part of the film committee, set out to make a small project to expose the theories learned into practice. My group went above and beyond what had been required or expected from us. It was a bittersweet experience. I loved it when we were actually doing it, but I hated waiting and seeing how things played out when I could do no more.

I guess God's main purpose with allowing me to join the project had been to teach me two things: Patience and Group Work. Both things I still need a lot of training in. I don't have lots of patience; I want things to work how I want them when I want them. And my anxiety plus my OCD have made the whole needing to be patient just not great. I used to be the kind of person that went ballistic if the schedule was not followed if the plan was discarded.

This project forced me to give up control, even when we all wanted to make things work somethings like traffic, weather or the light of day simply were not with us. I slowly started to relinquish control, but it would take a pandemic for me to finally learn that things cannot always go as I wish. Thankfully, Jesus started before hand with those lessons, exposing me to the loss of control so I would not freak too hard when things became more real.

In terms of patience, which went hand in hand with the whole needing to just let things play out as possible. The plan we had made at the beginning of the project was completely scrapped once we begun.

Preproduction took a bit longer than expected; as a result, the production schedule was delayed and finally postproduction had to be sped up and mainly invisible to me.

I got to produce the short film we made, a short film that after all the hard work, blood, sweat and tears ended up being recognized by a Dutch film fair. Yes, I was a producer, but the project was small and funded by all of us involved. We did and gave our best, often sleeping piled on top of each other in a corner while we waited for things to be set up. But when it came to postproduction none of us, but the director was involved. We were gracious enough to have the help of the director's friend to edit the footage. The end result was better than I could have expected.

The school later on wanted to accredit themselves with the work but to be completely honest the whole thing took off because of the hard work and passion of all of those involved. Every single one of us gave it our all and because it was a small student project this meant we were all very much united through the whole process, doing everything.

The whole thing was amazing, a peek inside into what being involved in the world of film making would be. Albeit of course on a way smaller scale.

I got to do it, I got to live my dream and although I loved it all, once it was done, I felt exhausted.

Celebrations were in order when the film premiered, I rejoiced with my beautiful co-workers and that night will forever live with me. Those moments were so special to me, and I am so thankful to God for allowing me to live them. I thank him for allowing me to live my dream even if briefly.

Meeting the Real Jesus:

2018 - 2019

Once I sat down in that church, the pastor began by welcoming everyone. Welcoming the congregation, thanking them for making time in their busy lives to come and worship God. Thanking them because God had given us another day. God had given us our church. God had provided the place and now we could be there and praise Him.

He carried on welcoming all the new faces, asking those of us who were first coming to please raise their hands. I was surprised to see more than a handful of raised hands. And where those hands were raised, everyone in the community turned in their seats to welcome them. They shook hands with us, asked us how we were, some even asked us to join for lunch later on the day. They even extended an invite and opened the possibility for us to join a bible study group. They looked so genuinely happy, filled with blessings, happy to be there and to be with God.

Those emotions were living, they were alive and loud in that school auditorium. They were the greatest way for God to receive me into his family. I genuinely had a prodigal daughter welcome into His love. The joy that exuded of those people, the certainty and the confidence with which they held onto God in all aspects of their life began to transform me that very day.

Even before the preacher began to preach, all of that weight I had been carrying had been lifted. I felt wholly held and loved. I felt safe and protected. I felt like finally I would not be alone. I had been praying to God for help. To help me find purpose, He of course already knew what it was, mainly to be His. He knew how stubborn I was, he knew who I was and how to reach me. He placed me where I was, fifteen minutes away from the perfect church for me. And slowly he started healing me, beginning with my issue of loneliness.

For so long I had felt alone and afraid. That first Sunday I had gone from having no one to having an entire family. I went from having no clue how I would spend my Sunday to having not just lunch plans but also dinner plans. I went from filling my days with study plans and study groups to joining bible study groups and prayer groups. My life completely flipped.

I willingly stepped into that new life, desperately so. My issue had been solved. God showed me how quickly and awesomely he answered those prayers I had not even known how to put into words. God saw into my heart, he saw my misery and worked to heal me. He showed me Himself first, he performed a miracle. He showed me his awesomeness first, practically thrust it in my face so I had no doubts whatsoever about who He was for. From that miraculous Sunday when God spoke to me and told me I was not alone, he would not abandon nor forsake me; My whole life changed.

You see, prior to that Sunday my understanding of Holy Trinity had been conversational at best. My understanding of God had been essentially thinking of Him as this mean and stern father, with very little patience and a predisposition for punishments.

I had grown up catholic through my parents' teachings, but I bet they were Catholics themselves for the same reason. Again, nothing wrong with that. The issue was that as an anxious person I could never be content with simply doing things, I love knowing why. I could not for the life of me figure out why we were Catholics. Not after I had learned of all the other options available to relate to him at a young age.

I was confused to say the least, confused as to why we had all decided to live like that. I'd lived with that question in me since Brazil, since I did my first communion while internally struggling with myself. Throughout the whole process I felt like an impostor, I did believe in God…just not the God they talked about. I could not understand how confessing all my sins to another human being would connect me more to a God, a supreme being. It was all very confusing. And anyway, wouldn't an all-knowing God already know all of them?

I stayed at the margins of religion. Yes, I wanted connection with God but not the way that they told me, not through their required procedures.

I felt in me that my place was not there, I did not belong in a religion but because it had been all I'd known and something my parents strongly felt about, I stayed.

What really helped was going to university, even though the first year was an emotional burden for the most part. Jesus still began to truly speak to me then, not at church but in my history of art classes. Weird right? I honestly think it was brilliant. Perfect for who I was then. I've always been a big fan of cause and effect and so naturally history has always called out to me.

As a student of art criticism when it came to defining what art was, we had to first look at its history. And since art in itself is such an arbitrarily big concept the next best thing was to simply study human history. Yes, we mainly focused on Europe and the East, but it was precisely in those lessons that I began to be transformed.

It absolutely perplexed me when my history of art teacher started citing the bible as a historical source. Everyone else seemed absolutely unphased about that but for me it was like grabbing the shroud of Turing and calling it an invisibility cloak. My curiosity was spiked, and I remember starting my own little research on what exactly was the bible.

It was enlightening, no pun intended, discovering the history of the bible itself. The fact that it is not a book but a book of books, written by multiple authors all seamlessly connected by a single theme: Jesus.

It sounded outlandish, the concept that a series of books written over thousands of years, in different places and over many generations could all be speaking about the same man. It just didn't make sense. Still, I learned a lot. All those facts became engraved in me, and it allowed me to start seeing Gods greatness even if I did not fully understand it yet.

The next big step was, as I've mentioned in the previous chapter, finally going to church. Once I was actually there, sat between all those beautiful souls who welcomed me with open arms once again my old friend the bible popped up.

In mass, those around me and seemingly everyone at church pulled out their bible to follow along to what was being preached. I did the next best thing and started looking up the verses on my phone.

I mean just think about it, think about how awesome Gods word is that it has not just survived generations but now also the modern era. Even to the degree that we can easily access it on our phones practically taking it with us wherever we go.

Yes, I did hear and receive the message that was being preached that day but for the most part I simply observed others around me. Observed how everyone seemed not just eager to follow along on their bibles but also noting on it like I did with my favourite novels as we went.

At the end of the service once all had been said and done and I had already been cordially invited to a bible study, I was asked if I had a bible or if I needed to borrow one. What an odd question that seemed, to have your own personal bible. A full mammoth book of books. I of course said I didn't but told them not to worry because I would figure it out.

Honestly, the whole experience of buying a bible was comical. It felt extremely weird to look up bible book shops only to discover the bible is actually the best seller of all times. Discover that for the most part bibles could be easily found in all book shops but there were different versions recommended and only found in Christian bookstores.

Different versions? I mean I had sort of already gathered that different translations of the bible existed what with the constant moving throughout the world and still going to church. Finding out that different versions or interpretations of the bible existed both blew my mind and complicate the whole purchase process.

Eventually I got around to investigating more about these different versions but that Sunday night I was short on time. So instead, I noted down the address of the cutest Christian store near me, gosh I love that store and also pray one day I can open my own because it was so wholesome and full of good vibes. Anyways, I allotted time on my busy schedule to go to the store and pick up a bible before the bible study on Wednesday night.

Stepping into the store the first time was daunting. I felt like everyone was looking at me, knowing I did not belong there and waiting for me to leave. I pushed through all those doubts, my curiosity was bigger than my fears and somehow, I made my way to the back of the store were all the bibles were. Why the back of the store I don't know.

But the vibe of the place was immaculate so I don't really think they should change anything.

The wall of possibilities was massive, I spent all the time I could pulling out bible after bible and reading the blurb. I know it sounds silly because they all essentially tell the same story, but the structure was what was different. Each edition focused on different elements, each one clearly set for someone with a little more knowledge than me. Someone already with a plan in mind on what next move to make in their faith journey.

In the end all the choices overwhelmed me but not wanting to leave defeated I simply picked up the smallest edition which was just a pocket bible with a pink cover and called it a day. I did not even check the version until I got home; I'd picked the Christian standard bible which I honestly think was God helping me pick because any other version would have been mad confusing.

As the overly eager student I was I attempted to begin reading the bible. I got as far as Genesis 4 before I gave up all together on reading any more. Still, I was curious about this so-called link between all the books and decided to carry on studying the best way I knew how: The internet.

Firstly, I looked up the story of the gospel, trying to understand what it was. It surprised me how little I knew about what I had called my faith for so long. Learning only days after my first church experience who God was, who Jesus was and how in fact the story of the bible was all connected.

I mean I had done my catechism; I had read all the little booklets they had given us, but no one had ever explained to me what my faith was actually based on.

My desire to learn more just amplified the longer I spent looking up the bible.

Secondly, I looked up how exactly it was that all those stories were linked. The bible project is a God sent and was an incredibly fun way for me to learn about this link.

Yes, I had gone unprepared but welcomed nonetheless to meet God in His own house. Now God had worked furiously in me in those short few days and equipped me with enough knowledge to give me the confidence to go to bible study. Yes, I'd probably be the most clueless of the bunch, but I was certain that my desire to learn would reveal to everyone how much I belonged.

I became one of those friends who always comments or asks in the group. My group was awesome, another incredible gift from God to reveal His love to me. My 2:2 group, named so after the verse of Colossians 2:2 "I want their hearts to be encouraged and joined together in love, so that they may have all the riches of complete understanding and have the knowledge of God's mystery--Christ."

United we were, Jesus worked in our eclectic group to intertwine us with His love through His word. 2:2 became my new family, and I was their rebellious child, being the youngest with God clearly showed but they still welcomed me.

From my part I eagerly joined them, wanting to absorb more and more of the awesomeness I was getting to know as God.

Reborn: June 2019

I gave my life to Jesus in June 2019. By all accounts I am still a baby with him, but the amazing work he has done in me has strengthened my faith beyond what I thought possible. Soon I joined the church missionary groups, eager to serve my all-loving God.

I became a part of the welcoming committee as well as the cafeteria committee. Those were the happiest moments of my existence. Yes, I still felt loss and uninspired in my studies, unsure if that had been the right path. But when Sunday morning came, I woke invigorated.

I had a purpose, one that made me whole and happy. Welcoming my fellow brothers and sisters in Christ with open arms and a big genuine smile on my lips to praise the King was my thing. It still is my thing; I don't think people understand how incredibly awesome it is for me to share what I learn. Not just about Christ but the world, everything that is new and explained to me is like a shiny new opportunity for me to share. You see I still love learning and sharing what I learn but when it comes to sharing what I learn about Jesus I feel whole and happy.

Sharing His awesomeness allows me to reflect and remember all His goodness while still praising Him. Just reflect on this very book you are reading. This entire experience has been enlightening and painful, but nonetheless beautiful.

Writing this book is my biggest act of faith, writing it has been tough and liberating. Praying it actually gets published and becomes successful in showing His glory is part of the process. I do pray it reaches the hearts of all who read it, whether that be only one reader or thousands.

Jesus didn't just turn over my life but gave me an entirely new one. New, there has never been anything like it. And while I still cling to my old one it is so refreshing knowing that I have a brand-new life in Him.

Second Year of Uni

August 2019 – March 2020

'What a freaking rollercoaster of a year', is how I would describe my second year of studies abroad. Beginning with the fact that I began the year as a new proud and loud daughter of Jesus, transforming my life by doing it from a whole new perspective. And ending with the very awful and life-changing pandemic.

Truly now I see how fast God gets to work in those who truly seek him, although I would have like it without all the struggles. Then again, all good teachers know that the best way to ensure the student has learned is to test them. So yeah, I got tested hard!

June 2019, I gave my life to Jesus and that Summer I spent entirely happy to be part of the big family of God. I was in cloud nine and I had, at that point, a massive desire and longing in my heart to turn others around me to Him.

When I returned home, I tried in all the wrong ways to push my parents and family to follow Him. I felt an urgency to this calling, and I also took it the wrong way by thinking it was all up to me. It is, in fact really not about me at all, Jesus has done all the work. The best way I can share Him with others is by simply sharing my life.

Once I returned to school, I did begin with the new mindset Jesus had given me. But soon enough I fell back into the old traps.

It was hard because at this point in my studies we were finally focusing on critiquing which had been my desired field all along. But at the same time, I did not feel whole. It was weird, finally getting to the point I had been working tirelessly towards and feeling nothing.

I tried and tried, as antecedent in my life showed I clung to those old dreams. I fought for them and gave my all again to my studies. I submerged myself into my studies and all I saw

Admittedly I loved it all because as I have said I do love learning. But it was at that moment in my life that I began to realize that what I loved was the learning, the thought of probably doing that as my living was odd, it didn't fit into this new me. I specifically recall telling one of my peers in one of our film classes how I wished with all my heart I could just be paid to learn. The thought of having to apply my knowledge later was odd now.

I mean, don't get me wrong. To this day if you ask me, I will tell you I am a film and theatre critic. Just not in the preconceived sense of the word. I watch things and I give you my opinion on them. I even have a blog, albeit quite neglected now. There I upload my reviews on what I have seen, read or generally consumed for entertainment. These days most of my reviews are book related and circulate the #booktok realms on Tik Tok.

The Pandemic:

March 2020

Things really took a turn when this new scary virus called COVID started to appear everywhere in the news. To say fear clung to all students would have been putting it mildly. No one knew what was happening, no one understood the severity of the matter. The university obviously had had no previous experience with a phenomenon of that magnitude.

The whole thing truly began to spiral downwards in March. Despite all of us following the news around the world and seeing how it had slowly started to spread after new year's, it was only in March that all went down.

I remember being really confused because all of my friends and peers over in Europe were worried about what this new virus meant. They fully understood the severity of the matter. I travelled in December to London to visit one of my school friends and even then, I remember all her peers worriedly chatting about the virus. But during Christmas and New Year's while back home in Mexico no one seemed to care.

It was literally a world of difference.

March came around and that was when I knew that I could not take my family's understanding be my base reaction guide.

Students took a stand on the matter and actually refused to show up to classes until the school took preventative measures. I of course could not afford such luxuries seeing as I was a foreign student and my parents had been making a sacrifice to allow me to study abroad. I'm also quite convinced I did contract COVID way beforehand since I had a real strong cold from December to March. Like really, really strong. That also didn't help once the panic began…I showed up to class anyway.

By the middle of March, the Dutch and European governments had finally begun to take preventative measures. Borders between countries were being closed down, international travel had begun to close, and transportation begun to shut down. Paired up with that, in my small city of Groningen the city decided that all unessential shops would close, the university would shut down and studies would be moved online.

I mean yes it was all scary, but it was also very comical seeing everyone line up for hours outside of coffee shops, aka weed dispensaries, to buy products in bulk for what everyone thought back then would just be a two-week break. The videos of those trips on Tik Tok are actually really funny.

I remember it perfectly, on the second week of March I along with other three students were the only ones showing up to classes. By Thursday of that same week, I had already worn my parents down after multiple calls and convinced them to fly me back home. Thursday night, the Dutch government issued a decree telling everyone that come Friday night the country would begin shutting down its borders, shops and schools to have everyone quarantined for the foreseeable two weeks.

By Friday night I had for the most part locked myself inside but that feeling of the world as we knew it ending permeated the air. All students went out and partied out like it was their last night on earth. I went out too but to the cinema because that had always been my comfort place, and this too was shutting down. I watched three films that day. I am so pleased I did because even though the world did not end, that whole era was done.

By Saturday everyone was fleeing the city, either by driving back home to their home countries or driving to their home city. Foreign students paid triple the price for taxis to drive them all the way down to the airport in order to avoid public transportation.

Come Sunday I left the city and made my way down to Amsterdam on one of the last trains. Once in the hotel at night the news confirmed the country's public transport was shut down and people were only allowed to leave their home for necessary trips.

I stayed as long as I could in the hotel, waiting out in the safety of my room before having to go out to the airport to fly home on that Monday.

To be completely honest, the Netherlands was not prepared for the virus at all. The weeks leading up to the event I had been going out to every shop I knew and asking for masks and found none. That Monday afternoon I left the hotel room armed only with a scarf and little sanitizing kit I had made.

Surely, I looked like a massive germophobe to everyone at the airport. I sprayed, wiped down and cleaned every surface I touched. I even took my time to clean down my airplane seat quickly but thoroughly. It did nothing in the end as the annoying teen sitting next to me kept on using me as a head rest the whole trip, even though I asked her to please keep her distance multiple times.

When I arrived, I locked myself in my room for two weeks, fully aware of how awful the virus was. The magnitude of its severeness finally hit news broadcasters worldwide. Even though my parents and family saw it, the virus had not yet reached Mexico fully and they did not understand why I kept away from them for two weeks. During those weeks, the virus finally arrived in the Americas.

Depression and Necessary Hard Changes:

2020

The whole thing was awful. Not just from my personal experience, Fleeing the Netherlands and having to carry on my studies online from the other side of the world. No, it was awful to see how horribly it hit everyone who was exposed to it. In those early days, contracting COVID was as good as getting a death sentence.

Hearing my parents getting call after call after call of family member passing was awful. Seeing the news and hearing how the number of deaths rose every day was awful.

Understanding that my own underdeveloped country did not have the manpower required to address all the cases resulting in the deaths of millions was awful.

Seeing my political leaders lie about the gravity of the situation was awful.

Seeing fear and misunderstanding cause many to attack and murder nurses and doctors was awful.

All of it was horrible. Made so much worse because my whole life had completely changed from one second to the next. Depression hit hard but I did not feel it as such. It was weird because it was the first time that depression as everyone knows truly consumed me.

I had no desire to do anything at all. I was uninspired and I could not see at all how to carry on with life. Existence was painful and all I wanted to do was sleep all day. I ate all my feelings. Anxiety convinced me my life was over.

You see, that control I had loved so much had been ripped from me. That year, God truly humbled me about who in fact was in control of my life. Realizing it would take a long while yet. The good news is now, as I write this book, I understand more why things had to happen that way. Yes, my God is good and always has perfect timing.

Returning to Mexico

March 2020

Returning home was an incredibly awkward experience. I had, despite suffering through most of it, been living alone for two years. I had gained my independence and had started to form a life of my own.

When I moved back, I once again became dependent on my parents to do everything, and I too had lost all ability to go out as I pleased. Yes, a big part of that was because of the pandemic, but part of it had a lot to do with returning to Mexico.

I had from a young age begun to understand the fundamental differences between Mexico and any other country I found myself in. Where in Europe I could generally take on adventures on my own, in Mexico leaving home alone as a woman represented an enormous risk.

My dad doesn't like to talk about it, he thinks I am hating on Mexico, but I don't see it like that. As I've mentioned I love Mexico, and still, I know it's not perfect. It needs a lot of work. The cases of femicide increased a lot during the pandemic; women who had previously depended on their husbands leaving for work for a much-needed break where now imprisoned with their aggressors. Crime rates rose and carry on being high because of the inflation caused by the pandemic.

And so, I sheltered myself at home with my parents. Not only could I not leave the house, but it would be extremely unwise to do so.

Yes, 2020 was hard. One of the cornerstones of hope that remained was God.

At first, like any young child I fought with Him. Asking Him to please enlighten me as to how exactly all of what was happening was any good. How exactly did His plan work out for me? I was angry.

Slowly though, God revealed part of His plan for me. My life as I had known it had ended, all I had planned and dreamed, died. Of course, I mourned it, a lot more presently than ever before. Amid all that struggle God met me once more.

Attempting to cram all His healing and teaching here would be unfair, I would not properly serve Him. I will write another book, one that exposes this new life I began with God in that storm. For now, I will finish telling you about my old life.

2020 was eventful. No one can deny that. Whatever way it was you lived it I do pray you overcame it. I pray that if you are currently still healing from it that what I shared here may have inspired you. Inspired you to find your true self. Once you've found your true self, don't let them go.

Remember life is a gift, live it and enjoy it. Make the most of every opportunity, live with purpose. And remember, even if you are still figuring it out, you still have a purpose. Finding it out may take some more time for some than others. Life is not a race, don't rush. Instead pace yourself, life is long but only you can decide how you react to it.